I0446555

Hey, everyone!

Thank you very much for taking the time to purchase this guide. I'm so excited for you to get your new job. You've worked extremely hard to get to this point! I know you are ready to put all that hard work you did in nursing school into practice, and you may be wondering, "how do I start this process?"

I remember how nervous (yet excited) I was to get my first nursing job. When I got the job, I was so elated! However, when I switched positions years later, I had to go through all the excitement and nervousness again with resume submission, interviewing, and so forth.

In this guide, I'll share all of my tips to help you get that job and advance in your nursing career. I'll explain step-by-step how to create a resume and cover letter, obtain letters of recommendation, things to include in a nursing portfolio, how to prep for the job interview, tips to transition from student to new nurse, and much more!

As a side note, I've also included some reference sheets to help you remember lab values, antidotes, and medication abbreviations and routes.

Finally, don't forget about the bundle of resume templates and cover letters that are included with this guide. Now, with all of that said…

Connect with Me:

- **YouTube**-RegisteredNurseRN
- **Website**-RegisteredNurseRN.com
- **Instagram**-registerednursern_com
- **Facebook**-RegisteredNurseRNs
- **Notes & Merch**-RegisteredNurseRN
- **TikTok**-@registerednursern.com
- **Twitter**-NursesRN

Let's get started!

Nurse Sarah

Don't forget about the included resume templates and cover letters. You will need to download them separately.

The download instructions are in the last chapter of this book, along with answers to questions you may have about editing or downloading the templates.

Copyright & Disclaimer

Copyright Notice:

Disclaimer:

Other books:

ABG Interpretation

Notes, Mnemonics, & Workbook

by Nurse Sarah

64 pages of Nurse Sarah's illustrated, fun notes with mnemonics and step-by-step instructions on how to solve ABG problems.

90 arterial blood gas practice problems & 60 review questions to help you retain the material.

Fluid & Electrolytes

Notes, Mnemonics, & Quizzes

by Nurse Sarah

130 test questions with answers and rationales to help you retain the material

84 pages of Nurse Sarah's illustrated, fun notes with mnemonics & worksheets

Check out our other nursing resources, with more coming soon!

Labs to Know
for adults

Metabolic Panel

- **Glucose:** 70–100 mg/dL
- **Calcium:** 8.5–10.5 mg/dL
- **Chloride:** 95-105 mEq/L
- **Magnesium:** 1.5-2.5 mg/dL
- **Phosphorus:** 2.5–4.5 mg/dL
- **Potassium:** 3.5-5 mEq/L
- **Sodium:** 135-145 mEq/L
- **BUN:** 5-20 mg/dL
- **Serum creatinine:** 0.6–1.2 mg/dL
- **Total Protein:** 6.2–8.2 g/dL
- **Albumin:** 3.4–5.4 g/dL
- **Bilirubin:** 0.1-1 mg/dL (less 1)
- **ALP:** 40-120 U/L
- **ALT:** 7 to 56 U/L
- **AST:** 10-40 U/L

This blood test can be ordered as a **BMP (basic metabolic panel)** or **CMP (comprehensive metabolic panel)**. CMP will check everything a BMP does, but it also includes liver function tests (noted in red).

Drug Levels

- **Digoxin:** 0.5-2 ng/mL
- **Acetaminophen:** 10-20 mcg/mL
- **Carbamazepine:** 4-10 mcg/mL
- **Dilantin:** 10-20 mcg/mL
- **Theophylline:** 10-20 mcg/mL
- **Salicylates:** 15-30 mg/dL
- **Phenobarbital:** 15-40 mcg/mL
- **Lithium:** 0.6-1.2 mEq/L
- **Valproic Acid:** 50-100 mcg/mL
- **Vancomycin**
  - **peak** 20-40 mcg/mL
  - **trough:** 10-20 mcg/mL

Complete Blood Count

- **WBC:** 5,000–10,000 per mcL
  - CBC with differential: assesses **5 types of WBCs:**
    - **Monocytes:** (4-13%)
    - **Eosinophils:** (1-5%)
    - **Neutrophils:** (40-70%)
    - **Basophils:** (0.1-2%)
    - **Lymphocytes:** (20-40%)
- **RBC:** 4.5-5.5 million cells/mcL
  - RBC indices: further looks at RBC (size, amount of hemoglobin etc.)
    - **MCV:** 80-100 fl
    - **MCH:** 27-33 pg per cell
    - **MCHC:** 33-36 g/dL
    - **RDW:** 11-15%
- **Platelets:** 150,000–400,000 per mcL
  - **MPV:** platelet volume 7-10 fl
- **Hemoglobin:**
  - 12–16 g/dL **(female)**
  - 14–18 g/dL **(male)**
- **Hematocrit:**
  - 37 – 47% **(female)**
  - 42 – 52% **(male)**

If results on the CBC are abnormal, a peripheral smear may be ordered. This will look at the morphology (this means the form or the shape of the cell).

Cardiac Enzymes

- **Troponin I:** <0.04 ng/mL
- **Troponin T:** <0.01 ng/mL
- **CK:** 25-200 U/L
- **CK-MB:** 3-5% of total CK
- **Myoglobin:** 25 to 72 ng/mL
- **BNP:** <100 pg/ mL
- **NT-proBNP:**
  - <125 pg/mL <75 years old
  - <450 pg/mL >75 years old

Miscellaneous

- **GFR:** >90 mL/min/1.73m^2
- **Urine specific gravity:** 1.005 to 1.030
- **Ammonia:** 15-45 µ/dL
- **Amylase:** 40-140 U/L
- **Lipase:** 0-160 U/L
- **TSH:** 0.5-5 mIU/L
- **T3:** 80-180 ng/dL
- **T4:** 5-12 mcg/dL
- **Creatinine clearance test:** **females:** 85-130 & **males:** 90-140 mL/min

Coagulation

- **PT (prothrombin time):** 10-12 seconds
- **INR (international normalized ratio):** < 1
  - When a patient is taking the anticoagulant Warfarin, the INR should be **2-3**.
  - The INR level is calculated from the PT level.
- **aPTT (activated partial thromboplastin time):**
  - Normal: **30-40 seconds (not on Heparin)**
  - If the patient is on Heparin, the aPTT needs to be **1.5 to 2.5 times** the normal range.
- **PTT (partial thromboplastin time):** **25-35 seconds**
- **D-dimer:** **<500 ng/mL FEU or <250 ng/mL DDU**
- **Fibrinogen:** 200-400 mg/dL

Lipid Panel

- **LDL (low density lipoprotein):** <100 mg/dL (want it LOW)
- **HDL (high density lipoprotein):** >60 mg/dL (want it HIGH)
- **Total Cholesterol:** <200 mg/dL
- **Triglycerides:** <150 mg/ dL

Assesses risk for cardiovascular disease.

Blood Gases

- **pH:** 7.35-7.45
- **PaCO2:** 35-45 mmHg
- **HCO3:** 22-26 mEq/l
- **PaO2:** 80-100 mmHg
- **O2 sat:** 95-100%

Diabetes Screening

HbA1c: hemoglobin A1c
- **<5.7%** (no diabetes)
- **5.7-6.4%** (prediabetes)
- **>6.5%** (diabetes)
- **<7%** (target for patients with diabetes)

Antidotes to Remember

Anti: "against" + **Dote:** "to give" = "to give against"

Medication:	➕ Antidote:
Heparin (anticoagulant)	Protamine Sulfate
Warfarin (anticoagulant)	Vitamin K
Benzodiazepines (sedative)	Flumazenil
Opioids (controlled pain reliever)	Naloxone
Acetaminophen (OTC pain reliever)	Acetylcysteine
Beta Blockers & Insulin (beta-adrenergic blockers) (antidiabetic)	Glucagon
Digoxin (cardiac glycoside)	Digoxin Immune FAB (DigiFab)
Anticholinergic Toxicity (antihistamines, atropine etc.)	Physostigmine
Cholinergic Toxicity (organophosphates & carbamates: used in insecticides)	Atropine
Magnesium Sulfate	Calcium Gluconate
Cyanide Poisoning	Hydroxocobalamin
Ethylene Glycol	Fomepizole
Lead Toxicity	Succimer (oral) & Calcium EDTA (injection)
Iron Toxicity	Deferoxamine

Medication Administration
Routes & Abbreviations

Route/Abbreviation:	Meaning:
• PO	• by the mouth
• SL	• sublingual (under the tongue)
• BUCC	• buccal (in between cheek & gum)
• NPO	• nothing by mouth
• IV	• intravenous
• IVPB	• intravenous piggyback
• IVP	• intravenous push
• IM	• intramuscular
• ID	• intradermal
• subQ	• subcutaneous
• TD	• transdermal
• INH	• inhaled 
• IO	• intraosseous
• ETT	• endotracheal tube
• NGT	• nasogastric tube 
• PEG	• percutaneous endoscopic gastrostomy
• VAG (PV) or RECT (PR)	• vaginally (per vagina)  • rectum (per rectum)

Table of Contents

1 Creating a Resume (1-8)

2 Cover Letter (9-15)

3 Letters of Recommendation (16-18)

4 Nursing Portfolios (19-21)

5 Getting a Job (22-27)

Table of Contents

Table of Contents

10   Download Resumes and Cover Letters (75-84)

Chapter 1:
Creating a Resume

Are you ready to land that ideal nursing position? One of the best ways to stand out among your competitors is to have a top-notch resume that screams professionalism. Employers often look for candidates who can showcase their skills and achievements with a polished and sleek resume. But don't worry, with this guide, you'll be able to easily craft a winning resume that does just that!

What is a Resume and Why is it Important?

A resume is a document that summarizes your personal information, academic background, and employment history. It is only meant as a summary and should generally be no longer than two pages in length (one page is preferred).

The idea is to "sell" the hiring manager on your skills and qualifications without going into excessive detail. You want the manager to feel the need to interview you to find out more.

It makes sense to spend a great deal of time creating your resume's content because this is the very first impression the hiring manager will have of you. If you submit a resume riddled with spelling errors, you may not get the job. Therefore, create your resume with great care, and ask a friend or two to look over it when you are finished.

In addition, it is best to stick with a professionally designed resume because this will help you stand out from the crowd and will likely get the hiring manager's attention (in a good way). This guide includes our resume template bundle so that you can select a professionally designed template that fits your style.

Pre-Resume Preparation

In today's age, many employers are using social media outlets (such as LinkedIn, Facebook, Instagram, TikTok, etc.) to research job applicants. What does this mean for nurses applying for their dream nursing job? It means that you really want to take time to clean up your social media presence.

In addition, you'll want to tidy up your contact information that you will be including on the resume itself.

Here are some things to consider:

- **Make sure the pictures and posts that appear on personal social media pages are not offensive.** Some employers may see applicants as a liability if they cannot exercise some discretion in their posted pictures and content, and many nurses have lost their jobs as a result. Consider deleting or hiding any objectionable content.
- **LinkedIn is a popular career tool!** Many job seekers are now creating a LinkedIn profile to help connect with potential employers. If you plan to include your LinkedIn profile on your resume, now is your time to review it for accuracy.
- **Create a professional voicemail message.** Many people have messages on their voice mail that may be appropriate for friends but not appropriate for employers. Edit these messages for profanity and the use of inappropriate words so that potential employers are not alarmed when leaving a message.
- **Change email addresses that contain offensive wording.** No one wants to be judged unjustly by their email address, so consider creating a separate email address for professional contacts. For example, avoid an email address with words like "hot-mama" or "sexynurse" in it. Instead, opt to use something with your name or initials and perhaps some numbers in it.

In addition to the steps above, you'll also want to gather all of your paperwork and resources before you craft your resume. This may include the following items:

- **Past Employment Records:** You may have to dig around for old check stubs or look up information about your past employers so that you can list their contact information on your resume. You'll generally need the name, address, and phone number of your previous employers, as well as the length of time employed.
- **Certifications and Academic Achievements:** You'll also want to gather any certifications you've earned, a copy of your nursing license, and any academic information the new employer may want (such as transcript records or diploma/degree information).
- **List of References:** Including references on the actual resume is optional. If you choose to include references on your resume, some details you may want to consider including are:

- phone number and email address
- relationship
- years known

Even if you decide not to include references on your resume, you will want to compile a list of professional references in case the interviewer or human resource department requests them. These references could be a preceptor, previous employer, or professor. Avoid using relatives and friends.

- **Letters of Recommendation:** These letters are not typically submitted with the resume but may be requested by the interviewer or human resource department. For example, after I had my first job interview, the nurse recruiter contacted me and requested a few letters of recommendation. Thankfully, during my last semester of nursing school, I had contacted several professors to write a letter of recommendation for me. I was able to use these letters. If you are still in school or are recently graduated, consider contacting a few professors so that you can have these for future use.
- **Volunteer Information or Nursing Associations:** Now is the time to make a list of all of the volunteer work you've done, or any state or local nursing associations you've joined. This always looks great on a resume, as employers love to see that applicants are involved with the community.

Once you have all of the above information in place, you can begin to craft your resume.

How to Structure a Resume

Let's talk about how to structure your resume. First, I'll show you an example of a completed resume, and then I'll break down each section to give you ideas on what to include.

Remember, when creating your resume, it best to keep it one page in length (Only two pages if absolutely necessary).

On the next page is a completed resume template.

Natalie Alexander
BSN, RN

About Me

Example: Recently licensed nurse graduate with clinical experience seeking a nursing position on a medical-surgical unit. Possesses a strong drive to help others, excellent communication skills, and a strong focus on delivering patient-centered care. Add as many details as you would like and be sure it focuses on your talents and how you will be a great employee.

CONTACT

555-555-5555

nataliealex@email.com

California, USA

Linkedin.com/username

EDUCATION

- 2025-2029
  Bachelor of Science in Nursing (BSN)

East California University
5846 Northwest Street
Lily, CA 36988
- **GPA: 3.5**

SKILLS

- **Patient Care** ★★★★★
- **Phlebotomy** ★★★★☆
- **Communication** ★★★★★
- **Documentation** ★★★★☆
- **Punctual** ★★★★★
- **Team Player** ★★★★★

Professional Experience

- **Senior Clinical Practicum | 2028-2029**
Student Nurse
Smithville Community Hospital
Cardiac Progressive Care Unit
Worked under the supervision of a registered nurse providing care to patients with various cardiac disorders

- Assessing and planning patient care
- Implementing and evaluating ordered treatments and outcomes
- Experience includes:
  - titrating cardiac drips, wound care, medication administration, intravenous therapy, starting IVs, central line management

- **Clinical Placements | 2026-2028**
  - **Intensive Care Unit -Jackson Hospital**
    - August 2027-May 2028
  - **Medical-Surgical Unit - St. Marks Medical Center**
    - January-June 2027
  - **Pediatric Unit - New Valley Hospital**
    - January-June 2027
  - **Labor and Delivery – Vincent Specialty Hospital**
    - October 2026-January

Licensure & Certifications

Registered Nurse
California Board of Nursing
License Number: 0000000

Advanced Cardiovascular Life Support (ACLS)
Expires: 2035

References

Samantha Mathers	555-555-5555	smathers@email.com	Preceptor
Robert Crawford	555-555-5555	robcrawford@email.com	Manager
Heather Sams	555-555-5555	samsheather@email.com	Professor

Let's break down each section of the example resume template on the previous page, starting with the **header**.

Natalie Alexander

BSN, RN

About Me

Example: Recently licensed nurse graduate with clinical experience seeking a nursing position on a medical-surgical unit. Possesses a strong drive to help others, has excellent communication skills and a strong focus on delivering excellent patient-centered care. Add as many details as you would like and be sure it focuses on your talents and how you will be a great employee.

1. **Name:** Make your name prominent! You want to include it somewhere at the top and in a large font. Be sure to include your first and last name (middle initial too if your name is very common). In addition, add your credentials. The degree (BSN) comes first, and then the credential (RN).
2. **Picture:** This is completely optional. If you want to include a photo of yourself, use a professional head shot.
3. **About Me Summary (or Objective):** Use this area to highlight who you are, the position you are seeking, and a short summary of your skills and talents. This is usually around 3-6 sentences in length, and are sometimes written as brief sentence fragment summaries. Here are a couple of examples of things you could write:
   - Recently licensed nurse graduate with clinical experience seeking a nursing position on a medical-surgical unit. Possesses a strong drive to help others, excellent communication skills, and a strong focus on delivering excellent patient-centered care.
   - Nurse graduate actively seeking a labor and delivery position. Has passion for helping families bring their babies into the world. Possesses exceptional communication skills and a commitment to providing high quality nursing care. Loves working and collaborating with others and is always willing to go above and beyond for my team and patients.

4

4. **Contact:** Here is where you add your phone number, email, location, and any website or social media account you've created as an employment marketing page. In regards to location, you can include your entire address, but it's up to you.

5. Education: This is the section where you highlight your highest level of education. Therefore, if a bachelor's degree is the highest level you've obtained, don't include your high school education. You can also add your GPA (3.5 or higher) and any honors earned (cum laude, magna cum laude, summa cum laude). Don't forget to include the name and address of the institution.

EDUCATION

5

- 2025-2029
  Bachelor of Science in Nursing (BSN)
East California University
5846 Northwest Street
Lily, CA 36988
- **GPA: 3.5**

6 **Professional Experience**

- **Senior Clinical Practicum | 2028-2029**
Student Nurse
Smithville Community Hospital
Cardiac Progressive Care Unit
Worked under the supervision of a registered nurse providing care to patients with various cardiac disorders

- Assessing and planning patient care

- Implementing and evaluating ordered treatments and outcomes

- Experience includes:
  - titrating cardiac drips, wound care, medication administration, intravenous therapy, starting IV, central line management

- **Clinical Placements | 2026-2028**
  - **Intensive Care Unit -Jackson Hospital**
    - August 2027-May 2028
  - **Medical-Surgical Unit - St. Marks Medical Center**
    - January-June 2027
  - **Pediatric Unit - New Valley Children Hospital**
    - January-June 2027
  - **Labor and Delivery – Vincent Specialty Hospital**
    - October 2026-January

6. **Professional Experience:** This next section should outline work experience. Start with the most recent positions you've had. If you're a new nurse graduate, you may be thinking, "I don't have any nursing experience!" However, you do! You have clinical experience from school. Therefore, include your clinical sites and any practicums. Be sure to include the type of clinical experience, your role, facility name, and your duties.

Licensure & Certifications 7

Registered Nurse
California Board of Nursing
License Number: 0000000

Advanced Cardiovascular Life Support (ACLS)
Expires: 2035

8 References

Samantha Mathers	555-555-5555	smathers@email.com	Preceptor
Robert Crawford	555-555-5555	robcrawford@email.com	Manager
Heather Sams	555-555-5555	samsheather@email.com	Professor

7. **Licensure and Certifications:** In this section, you want to show you are licensed to practice in the state you're applying, and make sure your license number is easily visible.

You may be wondering, "I'm not licensed yet, so what should I do?" You can list your licensure as pending, and write when you are taking the Next Generation NCLEX exam. In addition to licensure, add any certifications that pertain to the job. Many applicants list basic or advanced life support certification (BLS, ACLS, PALS).

8. **References:** This is an optional section to include as discussed previously. If you do include this section, be sure to have the person's name, contact information (phone number and email address), and state your relationship.

SKILLS 9

- **Patient Care** ★ ★ ★ ★ ★
- **Phlebotomy** ★ ★ ★ ★ ☆
- **Communication** ★ ★ ★ ★ ★
- **Documentation** ★ ★ ★ ★ ☆
- **Punctual** ★ ★ ★ ★ ★
- **Team Player** ★ ★ ★ ★ ★

9. **Skills:** This is an optional section as well. If you decide to include this in your resume, add 3-6 skills that help you look qualified for the job you are seeking. For example, if you are seeking a position as a nurse on a cardiac floor, you may want to add some of the following skills:

- ECG interpretation
- Cardiac drip titration
- Cardioversion
- Pacemaker care
- Heart cath care
- Balloon pump management
- Cardiac assessment

In addition, you can give yourself a self-assessed rating based on your skills. Be honest, and avoid listing something you cannot do well.

- **Additional Information (optional)** – This is where you may include volunteer work or similar activities. Alternatively, you could add a section that lists information about desired salaries, etc.

Punctuality

★★★★★

Patient Care

★★★★★

Advanced Cardiovascular Life Support (ACLS)
Expires: 2051

VOLUNTEER WORK:

Habitat for Humanity
Assisting and coordinating projects

Chapter 2:
Cover Letter

The final step in completing the resume is adding a cover letter. Most hiring managers recommend adding one to your resume as the first page.

The cover letter should grasp the reader's attention. Its content is usually 2-4 paragraphs in length. Keep it short (one page only), specific, and well written. I always recommend nursing applicants create the resume first, and then summarize it in the cover letter.

Remember, cover letter templates are included with this bundle so that you can easily create one that matches your resume template.

There is an example of a cover letter on the next page. I will explain each section in detail. However, here are common things included in a cover letter.

- **Your Name and Contact Information**

- **Date**

- **Addressee:** This is the person who will be receiving your cover letter and resume.

- **Salutation:** This is where you actually address the human resource department or hiring manager.

- **Body:** This is where you are summarizing the reason why the manager should look at your resume and consider hiring you.

- **Closing:** This is the part when the letter is ended and you can specify that your resume is attached.

Natalie Alexander, BSN, RN

youremailaddress@email.com | 555-555-5555 | 555 Your Address Street, City, State 55555

December 19, 2024

Hiring Manager Name
5555 Hospital Address
City, State 55555
555-555-5555 (their phone number)
hiringmanageremail@email.com

Dear Hiring Nurse Manager,

I am responding to the full-time job listing posted on your website, examplehospital.com. I am especially interested in the day shift position on your medical-surgical unit.

I recently graduated with honors from Sample University, and I am a licensed registered nurse with the California Board of Nursing.

As a nursing student, I quickly discovered that I had a passion for working with medical-surgical patients. I worked on the medical-surgical unit at St. Marks Medical Center during my nursing clinicals. During this time, I gained valuable experience with providing patient care and learning how to work as a nurse.

I would love to be part of your nursing team at Sample Hospital. I have attached my resume to this cover letter to further detail my professional experience, education, and certifications.

Thank you for your consideration, and I look forward to speaking with you.

Sincerely,

Sign here (leave blank space)

Natalie Alexander, BSN, RN
Enclosed: Resume

1. **Your Name as the Header**: Your name should catch the reader's attention. Be sure to include your first and last name (middle initial if your name is common) and credentials.

2. **Your Contact Information:** Near your name, list your contact information. Include your email address, phone number, and home address.

3. **Date:** Write the date of when you are sending the cover letter.

4. **Hiring Manager's Contact Information:** This is addressed to the person who will be receiving your cover letter and resume. Therefore, write the hiring nurse manager's information in this section. Include their name, company address, phone number, and email. If you cannot find this information, address it to the human resource department.

5 Dear Hiring Nurse Manager,

6

I am responding to the full-time job listing posted on your website, examplehospital.com. I am especially interested in the day shift position on your medical-surgical unit.

I recently graduated with honors from Sample University, and I am a licensed registered nurse with the California Board of Nursing.

As a nursing student, I quickly discovered that I had a passion for working with medical-surgical patients. I worked on the medical-surgical unit at St. Marks Medical Center during my nursing clinicals. During this time, I gained valuable experience with providing patient care and learning how to work as a nurse.

I would love to be part of your nursing team at Sample Hospital. I have attached my resume to this cover letter to further detail my professional experience, education, and certifications.

Thank you for your consideration, and I look forward to speaking with you.

7

Sincerely,

Sign here (leave blank space)

Natalie Alexander, BSN, RN
Enclosed: Resume

5. **Salutation**: Introduce the content with a phrase such as, "Dear Hiring Manager" or "Dear Jane Smith."

6. **Body:** Keep the content short at about 2-4 paragraphs in length. Each paragraph should flow logically, be easy to read, and should be free from simple spelling or grammatical errors. Summarize your skills, and include your reasons for applying for the job. The purpose of the body is to give a short "summary" of the resume. Make it compelling enough for the hiring manager to want to read your full resume.

7. **Closing:** Close the cover letter by giving a closing statement such as, "Best Regards" or "Sincerely." After that, leave a blank area to sign your name, and then type your name below the signature area. You can follow up with the words, "Enclosed: Resume" or "Enclosure: Resume".

Making Copies of Your Resume and Cover Letter

When you've completed your resume and cover letter, it's time to print it and make copies.

You can print the resume and cover letter onto regular printer paper, but you can also buy a thicker paper made for resumes at a local business supply store.

Furthermore, it is best to print in color if you've selected a colored template. If you don't have a color printer, again you can have a local business supply store help you with this.

Once you have your resume and cover letter printed, attach the cover letter to the front of the resume. As a side note, if you decide to attach a letter of recommendation, place it after the resume. However, keep in mind most experts recommend not attaching it to the resume itself, but rather to have copies of these letters available if requested.

Go ahead and print out several copies of your resume/cover letter for distribution. You'll also want to keep an extra copy or two to take with you while you interview.

This is especially important for situations in which the employer requires an online application only (so they can have a copy of your resume on hand during the interview).

You should also create a digital backup copy of your completed resume on a flash drive or second storage device. It is also good to convert the completed resume documents into different file formats.

For example, if you save them in .docx, you may also want to export a PDF version. Most word processors have this functionality built-in, and all you have to do to convert to a PDF is to go to File☐ Save As☐ PDF (for the file type). On some software, you may have to click File☐ Export as PDF.

The great thing about the PDF format is that it is universal, and most everyone will have the necessary software installed on their computer to view the document, whereas not everyone may have the .docx software.

Where and How to Submit Your Resume and Cover Letter

Now that you finally have your resume and cover letter completed, you can begin to submit it to employers.

Since we live in the electronic age, most hospitals, clinics, and doctors' offices want applicants to submit their resume via a website.

For example, most hospitals post job listings on their website via a job board. This was how I applied for my first job. In this case, you will usually have to create an account with a username and password, and then you usually complete a profile section.

In the profile section, there will usually be an area for you to upload your cover letter and resume. When you submit your cover letter and resume, try to upload it in PDF format as I described above (or whatever format the employer recommends).

After you submit your resume in this way, the human resource department will forward your information to the hiring manager. The hiring manager will then review it and decide if they want to interview you.

However, submitting a resume in this way is not always preferred by some organizations. If you learn about the job opportunity in a newspaper or radio advertisement, the employer may prefer you fax, email, or mail your resume. If this is the case, you will need to follow their instructions on how to do this.

Lastly, you may submit your resume in person to employers. This used to be the rule of thumb when submitting a resume in the past, but the electronic age and pandemic challenges have changed that. In today's age, most employers prefer people submit their resumes electronically.

Some employers may request that you apply or drop off your resume in person. If so, you should follow these tips below:

- Make sure you are submitting it to the right person (the hiring manager or their assistant).
- Try to pick a convenient time to present it, avoiding lunch time or closing hours.
- Ask to speak with the hiring manager or human resource department, if possible.

14

- Optional: call to verify that a hiring manager received your resume.
- Dress professionally when dropping it off in person. You may even be given an interview on the spot, so be prepared for the unexpected!
- Make sure you bring an extra copy of your resume just in case.

In summary, you want to submit your resume everywhere you possibly can. In a later chapter, I will give you specific tips on how to locate and network with potential employers in your area.

Chapter 3:
Letters of Recommendation

Letters of recommendation, also known as references, can provide a competitive edge when applying for a job.

If a hiring manager is having a difficult time deciding on which applicant is best for the job, a letter of recommendation may help give you the edge over other applicants.

What is a Letter of Recommendation or Reference?

A letter of recommendation or reference is a letter that someone with authority (such as a previous professor, nurse, etc.) writes about you with the intent of "recommending you" to the person to which the letter is addressed.

It is similar to giving a basic "reference," but it is even better in the sense that it is a letter of reference "selling" why you would be great for the position.

Letters of recommendation can have a significant impact, so it's wise to establish a relationship with your professors or colleagues ahead of time.

This way, they'll recognize and remember you, and they will be more willing to write a smashing recommendation letter.

Remember, a personalized letter with glowing remarks from a professor or boss can make all the difference and set you apart from the rest.

What's Included in a Letter of Recommendation?

A letter of recommendation (or reference) may include some of your achievements, personality traits, skills, and/or qualities.

For example, if you request a professor to write a letter of recommendation for an application to a nursing program, it may include information about your GPA, your rank within your class, anecdotal information about how you excelled as a student, your attendance, as well as reasons why you'd be a great candidate for the program.

When you are applying for a job, your letter of recommendation may include things such as your level of nursing skill, how you've shown leadership among your academic peers or co-workers, exceptional clinical experiences, and reasons why you'd be great for the job position. Ideally, it should be very specific and offer a personalized touch for the greatest impact.

How Do You Request a Letter of Recommendation or Reference?

It is common for professors, deans, clinical instructors, and co-workers to write letters of recommendation for their peers or students. Most professors will already be used to them being requested, so if you are still in nursing school (or a recent graduate), then this is probably your best bet.

You should consider the best professor or person who could offer you a good recommendation. Try to choose a professor in which you really excelled in their class and got to know them on a more personal level. Alternatively, if you were at the top of your class, perhaps a dean or chairperson over the school or university would write one for you.

If you're already working as a nurse, then try to find a co-worker or former manager willing to recommend you. Regardless of whom you choose, be sure they have a positive view of you and can offer a worthwhile recommendation.

When you go to request the person to write the letter, it is also a good idea to include some basic information about yourself for their benefit, such as your transcript, your contact information (full name, address, phone number, email), what position you are seeking, the program/organization in which you are applying, etc.

You can do this in a formalized way, such as giving them a copy of your nursing portfolio, or you can simply give them a typed letter with your contact information and the basic information described above. This will aid the person in preparing the letter and give them some insight or direction when preparing it.

For my first nursing job, I requested letters of recommendation during my last semester of nursing school. I choose a few clinical instructors and a professor I really liked to write my letters of recommendation.

I contacted many of them through their school email. In addition, I tried to ask them before other students did as well so they wouldn't feel overwhelmed by all the requests.

Therefore, if you are still in nursing school, go a head and start requesting them. Keep them organized in a folder for later use.

When Should You Request a Letter of Recommendation or Reference?

While letters of recommendation are generally short (about a page or so), they do take time to complete. The person writing the letter may have to look up information (such as your GPA). They may also need some time to reflect on why you were a great student or why they feel they can recommend you as an employee.

It is a great idea to ask at least 4 weeks or more before you think you will need the recommendation. This should be enough time for them to write it without feeling too rushed.

If it is a very personalized recommendation, or if the person recommending you has an established relationship with the person who will read your recommendation, then you may want to ask them to address it directly to the person or organization. Otherwise, it is okay for it to be a general reference letter.

Should You Include a Letter of Recommendation or Reference?

Again, these letters are not always necessary, but they can enhance your employment prospects. It is best to use these letters when applying to positions in high demand.

If you cannot get a letter of recommendation/reference, or if you feel you haven't achieved anything worthwhile, then it is okay to include written references only.

Chapter 4:
Nursing Portfolios

Most nursing students and nurses create a nursing portfolio to help them keep track of their professional goals, accomplishments, competencies, and skills. This is similar to how you might imagine an artist who creates a portfolio to show their work and accomplishments to future clients.

Nurses keep a portfolio to show future employers who they are and what they have done. When trying to wrap your mind around a nursing portfolio, think of it as a scrapbook that contains everything you have done up to that current moment in your nursing career.

A nursing portfolio does not need to be confused with a resume. A resume is a piece of paper that shows the employer a summary of the nurse's education, other job experiences, references, and certifications. The portfolio is the supporting documentation of that information.

How to Create a Nursing Portfolio

Some nursing schools require nursing students to create a nursing portfolio as a part of an assignment. This is a great way to help the new nurse get started with creating their portfolio. However, perhaps you have never created one.

Keep in mind that if you are a new nurse (or nursing student), your portfolio will not be as in-depth when compared to a nurse who has been in the field for several years.

Before you start creating your nursing portfolio, you need to compile supporting documents. There is no right or wrong way to do this.

Also, you need to include information that highlights your competencies, educational achievements, and skills.

Below are suggested documents that are often included in nursing portfolios.

Common Items Included in a Nurse Portfolio:

- Resume
- College transcripts
- One-page essay explaining your personal values and beliefs about the nursing profession
- An outline of your plan for professional development with supporting documentation of activities and learning outcomes
- Health records, including immunizations and current physical
- List of volunteer positions with supporting documentation
- List of professional organizations/memberships with supporting documentation
- Your job description
- Performance evaluations
- Competency checklists
- Copy of your nursing license
- Certifications with renewal dates
- Samples of academic work, such as research
- Professional conferences attended with supporting documentation
- In-services attended with supporting documentation
- References and recommendation letters
- Peer/manager evaluations
- Lists of committees you are on and the type of work you have contributed to them
- Educational projects you have done, such as in-services
- Awards you have received

Tips on How to Organize a Nursing Portfolio

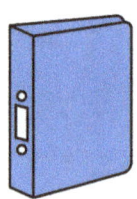

Once you have compiled all of the proper paperwork you need for your nursing portfolio, you need to place it into a three ring binder or a similar folder. It is a good practice to place the resume at the beginning of the portfolio because this has your name and contact information on it.

Try to organize your documentation in chronological order, if possible. For example, organize in-services based on the date they were completed. However, there is no correct way on how to organize your documentation. Try to organize it in a way that will make sense to the reader.

To help your portfolio look professional, be sure to label each section with binder tabs that can be purchased at most retail or office supply stores. Break each main section into a tab for ease in organization. For example, you may have an "immunizations" tab, a "certifications" tab, and so forth.

In addition, make sure to create a table of contents, and place in the front of the portfolio. Your nursing portfolio is your own creation, and it should reflect who you are as a nurse. Have fun with it! There is no right or wrong way to organize a nursing portfolio, but you should strive to make it as organized as possible.

Keeping a nursing portfolio will not only be helpful for potential employers, but it is also a great way for you to keep track of things yourself. Therefore, I'd highly recommend you create a nursing portfolio as soon as possible and continue adding content to it as you progress in your career.

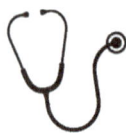

Chapter 5:
Getting a Job

Although there is often a high job demand for nurses, there can sometimes be a shortage of jobs in localized areas (or within certain specialties). In addition, while you can often get a job straight out of school with no experience (I was able to do this without any problems), sometimes it seems as if the only organizations hiring are those looking for nurses with at least 3-5 years of experience.

That's a catch-22 for the new graduate, isn't it? You need experience to get a job, yet you can't get experience until you get a job. Frustrating!

If you find yourself struggling to get a job after graduating from nursing school, or you want to change jobs but just can't seem to get hired anywhere—what should you do? I'm going to give you a list of things to do to help you get hired, but first let me tell you two things you shouldn't do: Don't panic, and don't quit.

It is easy to get frustrated and want to quit. You may start feeling as if you'll never find a job. I've had friends who started to panic, and I've known others who felt as if they couldn't get hired no matter what. Don't let those negative thoughts enter your mind. Instead, keep trying and you'll get there. Things will work out for you if you are persistent.

Below is a checklist of things you can do to help speed up the process of finding a job.

✓ Network While In Nursing School

If you are still in nursing school, I cannot stress how important it is for you to network with classmates, instructors/clinical teachers, and surrounding healthcare organizations. This is perhaps the single most important thing you can do to ensure you'll find a job right after graduation.

Even if you don't network throughout most of nursing school, make sure you put extra effort into networking during your senior year.

What do I mean by networking? Let me explain: When I say to network with classmates, what I mean is get to know some of your classmates. Develop a relationship with them, exchange emails, form study groups, etc.

Whether you like it not, you will work with many of these people. Some of your classmates may end up being your manager or close friends someday. A year or two after graduating, many of the people I went to school with had moved into management positions already. I've worked directly with many of my classmates in nursing school.

By making a few friends along the way, you can ask them to put in a good word for you with a hiring manager if you need a job. So make sure to network! With technology such as Facebook, email, and texting—this is easier than ever.

When it comes to networking with clinical instructors, this is where it can really pay off. I made a point to get to know my clinical instructors and preceptors on a personal level while I was doing my clinical work. This allowed me to build a relationship with them. During clinicals, I let them know I was very interested in working on a cardiac progressive care unit.

Because my preceptor knew how dedicated and serious I was about the job, she cheerfully recommended me to the manager on that floor. As a result, the manager hired me into the hospital's internship program before I had even passed NCLEX.

Her recommendation played a big role in helping me secure the position, and as soon as I passed NCLEX, I was a licensed RN and was able to make RN pay immediately in the same position.

So make 100% sure that you network with professors, classmates, and especially your clinical instructors and preceptors at the hospitals. This is especially true on the floors or in specialties in which you hope to work.

✓ Take Advantage of Job Placement Programs

Nearly all universities publish information and statistics revealing the number of their recent graduates who find jobs. Because they obviously want this to reflect well on them, they usually have a job placement service. Job placement services help recent graduates find jobs, which helps universities keep their job placement statistics high.

Nearly every established college or university will have a program like this, so it is a good idea to find out about what your school offers in terms of job placement assistance. This can be very beneficial, because this department will often have contacts with local employers and can help arrange interviews and meetings on your behalf.

It is a great idea to get in touch with this department during your senior year and to give them a copy of your resume (if possible) so that they can submit it to their contacts. By using these services, it can help you get your foot in the door and increase your odds of being hired as soon as possible after graduation.

Obviously, this only applies if you are still in nursing school (or a recent graduate), but don't overlook this excellent resource.

✓ Be a Nurse You'd Want to Hire

When you are working in your clinicals, you must be the type of nurse that you'd want to hire yourself. If you think about it, not only are you learning nursing skills, but you are also showing people what kind of worker you'll be once you graduate.

That's why you need to go "above and beyond" to make sure that you do your best on the job. This means doing the following things:

- Show up on time (ideally a few minutes early) to your clinicals each day.
- Obey all orders and take instructions seriously, without arguing or bickering about them. Do it cheerfully—even if you don't want to.
- Do not cause drama or say a negative word about anyone, even if others initiate the gossip. Instead, always be kind, polite, uplifting, and positive. Don't get dragged into "cliques."
- Practice the skills you need for the job. For example, if you want to work as a cardiac nurse, take time to study ECG rhythm interpretation, cardiac medications, and routine cardiac procedures. Nursing school really only skims the surface of these topics, and doing your own study will help you be more prepared.
- Communicate with your clinical instructor/preceptor and with the manager of that floor, and let them know that you really like the work. Express interest in working there upon graduation. Don't nag them; simply communicate with them and let them know how you feel. If they have an opening, and you've done a good job, you'll likely

get the job. If you don't communicate, then they may assume you don't want to work there after graduation. Remember the old saying: "The squeaky wheel is the one that gets the oil."

✓ Apply for an Internship Program

Another strategy you can use is to apply for an internship program (also called an extern program) with a local healthcare organization. This is a program where you can be hired-in and start working with limited duties as a nurse in training. Once you get your nursing license, you can then work legally as a nurse.

As I mentioned previously, this is exactly what I did. Because I had made contacts at the local hospital during my clinicals, and they had an intern program available, I was able to secure a position on that floor. This was great because I was earning money in the program, and once I passed my NCLEX, I was able to go to work immediately as an RN.

Many hospitals and other healthcare agencies offer internship programs. Companies often post these listings on their websites, through your university, or you may have to contact the human resource department directly to inquire about any potential internship program. If there is a certain organization you have in mind, find out if they offer such a program.

Either way, I'd highly recommend you take advantage of these programs. Not only can you make money (many of them are paid positions), but you will greatly increase your chances of securing a job once you graduate and/or pass NCLEX. You'll want to do this during your senior year or during your senior practicum.

✓ Attend Job Fairs

Another strategy you can use is to attend job fairs. Job fairs may be arranged and hosted by local employers, by your university, or both. I hear them advertised often on the radio where I live, and I know that my school hosted many job fairs.

You will typically want to dress professionally for the job fair, bring many copies of your resume and/or nursing portfolio, and be prepared to talk with several potential employers. Depending on how the job fair is planned, you may be speaking with many local employers or just one.

This is a great way to network with people, get business cards, and establish those important contacts. You can often schedule interviews with employers directly or at least drop off your resume, which may later lead to an interview.

✓ Searching for Jobs 🔍

If you fail to find a job using the other methods above, then you still have a few other resources available to search for jobs.

As I've mentioned before, most healthcare facilities will place job positions on their website directly. To search for these job listings effectively, make a list of all of the surrounding hospitals or healthcare facilities in your region. An online directory may help you compile your list.

Next, use a search engine to find the website of each healthcare facility. Nearly every hospital or healthcare organization will have a website. When you find the organization's website, there should be a link titled "Careers" or "Jobs." Click that link to browse their website for jobs. If there is no "Careers" or "Jobs" link, you can always contact them through the website to inquire about current job openings.

Aside from searching directly on healthcare websites, you can also check your local paper. Sometimes healthcare facilities will post a job in the local paper detailing a position available. So make sure to check the classifieds section of all local papers or publications.

As I mentioned in another chapter, it may be beneficial to create a LinkedIn.com profile. I've head about nurses who have created a public LinkedIn profile, and they were shocked at how quickly they began receiving job offers from nurse recruiters. This made their job search very easy because the job came to them, instead of them going to the job.

Lastly, don't forget to check other online resources. You can visit ZipRecruiter.com, Monster.com, Indeed.com, Simplyhired.com, and Careerbuilder.com to search for jobs based on various criteria. Most of these websites also allow you to upload a resume and create a profile.

✓ If All Else Fails, Be Prepared to Settle

If those tips don't work, and you are still struggling to find a job after a few months, then your best option may be to accept whatever nursing job you can take. Even though it may not be your dream job, it will give you the opportunity to earn experience (and an income).

Once you have 2-3 years of experience under your belt, you will have much more flexibility in your career, and you will be able to apply for more jobs (and possibly even be in a position to negotiate for a higher salary).

I like the way one nurse put it: "After 2 years of working as a nurse, you're considered experienced. After 3-5 years, you're considered an expert in the field."

Even though I was happy to get a job I liked after graduation, it wasn't exactly the most glamorous job in the world. In other words, it wasn't exactly my "dream job." Nevertheless, I was very thankful that I was hired immediately and that I could begin gaining experience and earning a salary.

You may have to settle for a job you don't like if the economy is in rough shape. In fact, you may even have to take a job you absolutely hate. However, keep in mind that you have your entire career ahead of you, and you will have many great opportunities to change positions and grow. There are truly so many possibilities within nursing!

✓ You Can and Will Get Hired If You Keep Trying

Even though you may have trouble, you will eventually be hired. I'd highly recommend you prepare long ahead of time, before you graduate nursing school (or quit your current job). It's always beneficial to be prepared for job hunting.

Make sure you have your resume and/or nursing portfolio together, and start making a list of the places you'd like to work. Use the tips mentioned above, and you'll greatly increase your chances of being hired.

Chapter 6:
Leaving Your Current Job

Perhaps you already have a job, and you're wondering if it's time to get a new one. Did you know that according to the Bureau of Labor Statistics, people born between 1957 and 1964 have held an average of 11 jobs from the ages of 18 to 44?

(Source: "NLS FAQs." U.S. Bureau of Labor Statistics. U.S. Bureau of Labor Statistics, n.d. Web. 26 Sept. 2013. <http://www.bls.gov/nls/nlsfaqs.htm>.)

Statistically speaking, people tend to change jobs many times during their life. There are many reasons why people change jobs, and here is a short list of the common reasons:

If you have ever switched jobs, chances are you probably chose to leave your position due to one of the reasons above. I remember suffering from the symptoms of burnout with my first nursing job. I started to sense that it was time for me to move on, but I was afraid to leave because I was comfortable.

However, after three years of working on that particular floor, I decided it was time for a change. Nevertheless, I am thankful for the experience I received with my first nursing job because it taught me how to be a nurse, and it gave me a much-needed income at the time.

Burnout among nursing professionals is very high due to the nature of the work. It is important that you are able to recognize the early signs of burnout before you start to feel miserable and question if nursing is for you. Not only will you experience the repercussions of burnout—your patients will as well.

One thing I love about the nursing profession is the incredible diversity of job settings you can enjoy as a nurse. There are so many job opportunities and specialties out there, and you're bound to find something that will re-energize you and make you excited about being a nurse.

Signs it is Time for a New Job:

- You find yourself wanting to call-in all the time to avoid having to work
- On your days off, you stress about work and having to go back
- You're apathetic towards your co-workers and patients
- You are constantly complaining at home to your spouse or friends about how much you hate your job
- Your health is declining. Some examples of declining health may include high blood pressure, migraines, stomach ulcers, weight gain/loss, anxiety, insomnia, bouts of anger, and depression
- Your attitude at both home and work is negative, pessimistic, and bitter
- You have trouble sleeping the night before you go to work
- You are too exhausted on your days off to relax and have fun

What should you do when you realize it's time for a new job? Be proactive, and start looking for another one as soon as possible. Go ahead and get your resume in order, and begin collecting references. Once you do that, you can begin submitting your resume to healthcare facilities in your area.

Sometimes, it can take months to find a better job. I waited almost to the point of desperation by the time I decided it was time for a new job, so I don't recommend that you wait that long!

I wish I had been more proactive in looking for a job when I started to feel the effects of "burnout." I also wish I had recognized my symptoms earlier. However, I knew I had to be patient in switching jobs because I did not want to go from a bad situation to an even worse one.

After a couple of months of being selective, I found a job that I loved. As the saying goes, "Good things come to those who wait." When you decide it is time for a new job, start looking immediately, just remember to be very selective and patient.

How to Leave Your Current Job Gracefully

It is always a best practice to give your current employer at least two weeks' notice that you will be quitting your job (or more if they ask or require it when you were hired). Some companies may actually force you to sign an agreement stating you will give them a certain notice before quitting. Either way, the important thing is that you always give a proper notice, especially since nurses deal with life or death situations.

It doesn't matter how much you dislike your manager or hate the job itself. Don't skip this step. You should always give a notice and be professional in the way your present the notice.

The purpose of giving a notice is not just for the benefit of the employer, it's also for the benefit of your professional career. As a nurse who has worked closely with nurse managers (the ones who do the hiring), I have seen instances where nurses have quit by not showing up for work.

In other words, they did not give a notice before they quit and left for another job. They "just" quit by not coming to work. In turn, these nurses were not eligible for re-hire for many years, if ever, because of this unprofessional behavior.

Some employers (and I've heard of hospitals doing this) actually keep a "blacklist" of people who quit without giving a notice.

Here's the takeaway: Give a notice to your employer when you're sure you will quit. Don't burn a bridge. Giving a notice helps preserves your reputation as a responsible employee. In addition, don't forget that your new employer may ask if you gave a notice to your old employer.

How to Give a Notice

What's the best way to give an official notice or resignation to your employer? From speaking with many nurse managers, and being in the position myself as an employee who has switched jobs, sitting down and talking with your manager face-to-face is the best way to give a notice.

You should also give the manager an official letter at this time, which officially states your two weeks' notice (or the date of your resignation). This is the most transparent and professional way to leave a job. It isn't always the easiest way, but it is the best way. Even if it feels awkward or uncomfortable, make sure you handle the situation with class and professionalism.

In addition, let your manager be the first to know that you will be quitting. Wait to tell your co-workers until after you've given your notice to the manager, because gossip spreads fast. If you tell other people that you are going to quit before telling your manager, it will probably get back to your manager before you are able to tell them. What reasonable person would be happy about that?

Another way you can give your notice is via telephone. If you decide to do this by phone, you may want to warn your employer that you will be calling them ahead of time. Ask when a good time would be for them to talk with you. This will help avoid any interruptions. Avoid calling them up on a whim and giving your notice.

Even if you do give a verbal notice via phone, you still need to present an official written letter of resignation.

The Wrong Ways to Give a Notice:

- Text message
- Voice message
- Facebook
- YouTube or TikTok video
- Someone else does it for you
- A "noticed" notice (meaning, they "noticed" you never came back)
- Email*
- Letter*

*Email and letter can be used but not alone.

For instance, you can tell them face-to-face and give them a letter at the same time. A written letter and discussion face-to-face is the preferred method.

How to Let a Manager Know in a Face-to-Face Meeting

- Schedule a meeting with your manager
- Arrive on time
- Smile and be professional
- Bring a written copy of your notice

Here is how you can give your notice verbally to your manager:

> "I want to thank you for taking the time to meet with me. I called for this meeting because I wanted to let you know that I have accepted another nursing position, and I wanted to give you an official notice.
>
> In addition, I would like to thank you for the opportunity of being able to work with you and your team. I have learned so much during my time here, and I will always value this experience."

As you are speaking with them, hand them your official letter of resignation.

Remember to be polite and professional. The manager may ask you a few questions, so just be prepared to answer them.

I've provided a sample letter of resignation below. You'll also receive a template of this in .docx format (included in the download bundle).

This will be handy to keep, as you'll likely use it throughout your career.

To use the template, alter the text with your own information. You can change as much as you want.

Sample Written Notice of Resignation

Your Name
Street Address
City, State, and Zip
Phone/Email

May 15, 2024

Manager or HR Person's Name
Example Healthcare Corp.
Company Address

Dear [Manager's Name],

I am writing to inform you that I have accepted a nursing position at [Example Hospital] as a [nurse position], effective June 05, 2024. I am very excited about this new opportunity, and I know that I would have never been prepared for it without the experience I have gained under your leadership.

I value the time I've spent working with you and the entire team, and I want to thank you all for the opportunities you've given me. I will always be thankful for the time I've spent here.

I wish nothing but the best for you, the team members, and this organization.

Sincerely,

(Leave blank to sign your name here)

Type Your Name, BSN, RN

Chapter 7:
Getting a Job Interview

At this point, you've considered your job possibilities, submitted resumes/applications, and you have finally landed your first interview. Congrats!

Are you ready to start preparing for your interview? Let's take a closer look at what you can expect during the process.

Preparing for Interviews

Before you actually sit for the interview, it is a great idea to start preparing ahead of time. Here is a brief checklist of things to help you prepare:

- Prepare a copy of your resume and cover letter, and take along at least 2-3 copies.
- Take your nursing portfolio and any letters of recommendations (if applicable).
- Get a hygiene tune-up (haircut, clean/cut your nails, etc.).
- Buy a business professional outfit if you don't have one.
- Consider cleaning up (or make private) your Facebook, TikTok, Instagram, Twitter, and email address (as previously mentioned).
- Practice interview questions (see sample questions and answers later).
- Practice good interview etiquette (more later).

Common Interview Questions with Answers

I'll share with you some of the most common interview questions you can expect, along with potential answers. The interview questions may be phrased in a different way, but it is likely you'll be asked similar questions.

I highly recommend you review these interview questions and take time to personalize your responses. Rehearse it a few times with a friend or family member so that you will feel comfortable and natural, and have them throw you a few unexpected questions so that you can practice how you'll respond when you don't have a prepared answer.

"What's the hardest decision you've had to make recently (in nursing school or on the job)?"

When employers ask this question, they are trying to see how you will react when you are put on the spot. They are also trying to gauge what you perceive to be a difficult situation.

Therefore, try to think of a situation from a previous job that you found difficult, but then talk about how your decision was right. If you have never worked at a job before, think back to a time in clinicals when you and/or a preceptor faced a difficult decision.

For example, perhaps there was a time when a patient wasn't doing well, and your nursing intuition told you that something wasn't right. You had mixed feelings about calling the doctor to report it, but you went with your gut, and it turned out you were right. Here is a potential answer:

"During clinicals, my preceptor and I encountered a potentially life-threating situation with a patient who was presenting with signs and symptoms that were being ignored by the resident on-call. The patient was post-op from surgery that week, and it was the weekend. Therefore, the doctor who performed the surgery was unavailable, and a resident was rounding on the patient.

My preceptor and I suspected that the patient was internally bleeding from the surgery. We called multiple times, but the resident said that there was nothing wrong with the patient. We had to be stern and persistent with the resident, who eventually notified the surgeon about the issue. The patient ended up being rushed for emergency surgery because they were internally bleeding, just as we suspected.

This situation was hard because there was a chance we were wrong, but we cared more about the patient than being embarrassed by being wrong."

"How do you define great patient care?"

It's important for you to know that great patient care is a major focus for most healthcare organizations, especially since The Affordable Care Act instituted a system that financially rewards hospitals based on patient satisfaction surveys.

Therefore, it's important to emphasize that as a nurse, you're going to be all about the patient!

You might want to say, "I believe great patient care means that you are patient-centered, which means that you address their concerns and respond as quickly as you can to their needs. It means that you take time to educate them so that when they leave, they feel as if you took good care of them and would recommend your facility to others."

You might want to add personal anecdotes of how you've gone above and beyond for a patient in the past.

"Describe a mistake you made on the job (or in clinicals), and explain how you handled it."

No one likes to re-live their nursing mistakes, but you really need to go into the interview with an example of an honest mistake that you've made in the past. However, avoid mistakes that make you look incompetent or that would cause potential legal issues.

For example, mention a time you made a simple charting error that you were able to correct. Alternatively, perhaps there was a time when you collected a lab specimen, and the specimen became contaminated.

Be sure to include the details of the steps you had to take to correct the mistake, and how you learned how to avoid it in the future.

An example could be:

"Once I collected a lab specimen, and it became contaminated because I was in a rush. I had to apologize to the patient, and I informed my shift leader of the mistake. This mistake caused me to reflect back on how I can prevent this in the future, and it helped improve the way I collect lab specimens."

"Describe a time when a coworker or manager made you upset."

If you are asked a question like this, keep two things in mind:

- You don't want to come across as petty or dramatic.
- Don't talk poorly about your former coworkers or boss.

Instead, try to keep it as professional as possible, and think of something that affected patient care or the nursing team, such as a time when a coworker obstructed workflow for the team, arrived late, or didn't give proper report.

Be ready to address how you handled the situation, too. Here is an example:

"The nurses on our unit were failing to get regular lunch breaks. This was upsetting and affected the staff's job performance and morale. I presented the issue to the nurse manager, who quickly remedied the situation. We created a "lunch buddy" system for the team, and everyone was happy."

"Describe the most valuable constructive criticism a former manager or charge nurse has given you."

This question might also be phrased like this, "What's your biggest fault as a nurse?"

Think of something that you can improve on, but again, avoid saying something that makes you appear incompetent.

Try to include a personal anecdote or story, but stick with themes such as:

- You're a perfectionist
- You push yourself too hard
- You sometimes get emotional when a patient suffers

Finish your answer by saying that it is something that you have been working to improve.

"What attracted you to our organization?"

If you are asked why you want to work for that particular organization, you'll want to give a good, researched answer. Therefore, make sure that you do your homework, and research the organization a bit.

Each organization will have its own focus or motto. Look into the company's history, and incorporate that into your answer.

For example, if a company advertises a big emphasis on patient care, you could say something like this: "One thing I love about this organization is that you are really focused on patient care, and I love that; it's one of my strengths."

Furthermore, let's say the cardiac position you are interviewing for is at a hospital that is known as the leading cardiac hospital in the state. In your response to this question you can say something like this: "St. Mary's is known as being the state's top hospital in cardiac care, and I'd love to join this team. I know I can bring hard work and dedication to this position, but also learn and grow under the leadership at this leading hospital."

Here are some other things you can mention, if relevant:

- The company has a great reputation in the community, and you've heard great things from both patients and other nurses
- Perhaps the company has won recent awards or received positive publicity
- Perhaps the facility has Magnet status
- Perhaps the facility has a great training/teaching system in place
- Perhaps the company has many opportunities for advancement

"What's the most important quality a nurse can have?"

When asked this question, think about what it is that really drives you as a nurse, whether it's a hard work ethic, attention to detail, a love for helping people, etc. You might even want to think back to your grueling semesters in nursing school, and try to think about what it was that motivated you to get through so that you could work as a nurse.

For me, it's helping people. So, I would probably answer this question by saying, "While I think it is extremely important to have competence in clinical skills, the most important skill that a nurse can have is to genuinely want to help people get well and stay healthy."

How would you handle a rude physician or supervisor?

Here's how I would answer this question: "I would try to remember that you never know what is going on in a person's life that could be causing them to be rude. They could be having a bad day or going through a personal issue.

So, I'd try to maintain a professional attitude and overlook it. As the famous proverb goes, "A soft word turneth away wrath."

However, if someone has a consistent problem with being rude, then I'd confront them in a professional way, and if that didn't work, I'd talk to a supervisor or manager."

Why are you a good candidate for this job?

This is always a tough question, and you'll want to speak from the heart. Here are some things you might to incorporate into your answer:

- Any credentials you have earned
- Your passion or interest in that specific specialty or industry of nursing
- Your love for people
- Team player
- Punctual
- Strive for hard work and professional attitude
- Love learning new things and growing
- Experience and knowledge
- It can help me grow

More Interview Questions to Ponder (with Answers)

In addition, here are some more potential interview questions that you may be asked. As you read them, think of possible responses you can give the interviewer.

1. Do you find the field of nursing difficult?

"Yes, at times it can be difficult because we are dealing with life and death situations, which can be stressful at times. However, the difficult times can make us stronger and help us improve patient care."

2. Do you prefer working with others as a team or by yourself? Explain your reasons.

"I prefer working as a team. If a successful team is put together, amazing outcomes can be achieved. This benefits not only the patient but each team member as well."

3. Are you interested in advancing your current career someday?

"Yes, I am always interested in growing as a nurse, but first I'd like more experience in this specialty. I think this position is the best fit for me at this time."

4. Are you a self-motivated person?

"Absolutely! I love taking initiative and challenging myself to be better and to work harder."

5. How would you handle a situation where your replacement doesn't arrive?

"I would notify the person in charge and continue to do my job until help arrived."

6. What is the most rewarding aspect of being a registered nurse?

"The most rewarding part is knowing that the work I am doing is positively affecting the lives of others. There are many jobs out there where this is not the case. However, nursing (no matter the specialty) allows you to make this difference."

7. How would you handle patients who constantly complain?

"I think the reason most patients complain is because we are failing to listen to them and meet their needs. Therefore, I would sit down and listen to the patient's concerns and then work to find a solution."

8. What do you think is your biggest contribution to your patients?

"I think one of my biggest contributions is my desire to advocate for the patient and their families. My job as a nurse is to be a voice for them when they are unable to speak for themselves."

9. How would you handle a patient's family members who were unhappy with your care?

"I would try to collaborate with the patient's family members on how to identify why they're upset, and then I'd create a solution that would make them feel like they're getting the care they deserve."

10. How would you handle a rude physician, supervisor, or coworker?

"When people are rude, it's often because they are having a bad day. I would try to see things from their perspective and not provoke them to more anger. However, if the situation escalated, I would ask management to intervene."

11. How do you deal with stress while on the job?

"I go into every shift being prepared for the unexpected. I know that nursing can have times where it is very stressful, and this is why I would make sure I have a good network of coworkers and resources that can help me through those tough times."

12. What made you decide to become a registered nurse?

"Since I was young, I was always drawn to science and helping people. Nursing allows me to do two things that I love."

13. Are you affiliated with any professional nursing organizations?

Answers may vary, but you may want to consider joining a local or state nursing organization.

14. How has your nursing program prepared you for your career?

"The nursing program I attended provided excellent review in nursing theory and was able to combine that with a variety of clinical experiences."

15. What do you do in order to keep current with the latest nursing practices and findings?

"I participate in local nursing organizations and meet my continuing education requirements. I also subscribe to popular online nursing resources such as RegisteredNurseRN.com." (I'm just making sure you're still paying attention.) 😉

16. What do you think are the most important skills that a nurse can have?

"A nurse should have a desire to serve others, be proficient in their clinical skills, and be willing to work with their team to provide the best care possible."

17. What made you decide to leave your current position?

"I'm looking to gain experience in this specialty, and I feel like this facility has a great reputation in the community."

18. How do you handle emergency situations?

"First, I make sure that I stay updated on the latest protocols for handling emergency situations. When a situation occurs, I try to remain calm, focus on the situation at hand, and contact necessary resources for assistance."

19. What attracted you to our organization?

"This facility has Magnet status, offers cutting-edge, patient-focused healthcare, and is making a difference in the lives of people in this community."

20. How have you assisted coworkers in the past?

"A new nurse experienced a patient code. I assisted her with the patient by getting the crash cart as she began CPR. I remained with her until the code team arrived, and I offered emotional support afterward."

The Tricky Interview Question...

Many nurse managers are now asking specific interview questions about nursing care related to the specialty to which you're applying.

For example, if you're interviewing for a job in a cardiac unit, the nurse manager may ask you a question like, "If your patient complained of chest pain, what would you do as the nurse?"

I can tell you from experience that when you work on a cardiac unit, you're probably going to have at least one patient complain of chest pain during your shift. It is very common. That's just an example of a specialty-specific question. It could be anything related to nursing care.

If you're a new grad nurse, you probably don't have a lot of experience, so you need to make sure that you know exactly what type of unit you're interviewing for, because that will allow you to go back and refresh your knowledge on that particular area of nursing.

Let me give you an example of how you can prepare for this type of question (using the cardiac nursing example). You'll want to review common cardiac diseases such as:

- Heart Failure
- Myocardial Infarction
- Coronary Artery Disease
- Hypertension
- Heart valve disease
- And you'll want to be able to recognize basic dysrhythmias

You'll also want to be prepared to answer questions that deal with the following (again using the cardiac specialty as an example):

- Pre and post-op care for cardiac patients, such as heart caths, stress tests, and pacemaker placements (just the basics that you've learned in nursing school).

- Common medications used to treat those heart conditions, such as ACE inhibitors or angiotensin II receptor blockers (ARBs).

- Nursing interventions for cardiac patients. Let's say you have a patient with heart failure. Some of the nursing interventions would be monitoring intake/output, taking daily weights, monitoring their diet, and making sure it is low sodium and low fat, etc.

I've had several nurse grads tell me that they were asked a nursing care-specific question like this during the job interview process.

Therefore, you'll want to take some time to study up on the specialty for which you're applying so that you can nail that one type of question with confidence.

What if You Don't Know the Answer to a Nursing Scenario?

What if you are asked a question you don't know, and you have no idea what to say? Instead of saying, "I have no idea," here are some ways you can respond:

- You might want to ask the nurse manager to elaborate more on the scenario while you think of the answer.
- Begin by talking about what you do know about that area of nursing, and then shift to saying you'd consult with a fellow nurse or check the most recent protocols.

Try to avoid saying, "I don't know." Instead, show the nurse manager that you do know some things about the specialty and that you're willing to find out what you don't know.

What to Wear to Your Interview

You can't always judge a book by its cover, but oh, how people try! Whether we like to admit it or not, looks are important in our society. People will make all kinds of judgements based on your appearance.

The person interviewing you is going to judge every little detail about you (even if they do so subconsciously), and they will use these details to form an overall impression of you. Therefore, it is critical that you give a good impression.

Let's talk dress. Since you are applying to work in a very professional atmosphere (doctors, nurses, life or death, etc.), you want to wear **business professional dress** to the interview. Below are some suggestions for attire.

Dressy & coordinated
Not showing a lot of skin
Simple jewelry
Groomed hair style
Light or no fragrance
Skirts, suits, blazers
Neutral colors (not bright, attention grabbing)
Matching shoes that are closed-toe (no sneakers)

How to Behave During the Interview

Be sure to use good etiquette during your interview. You don't want to come off as pushy, rude, ignorant, selfish, or unprepared.

I can still remember a funny story that a nurse manager told me about an interview she once conducted. The nurse manager had scheduled an interview with a woman for a position on her floor. In this particular hospital, the human resource (HR) room was a very long walk from the floor in which this nurse manager worked.

So the nurse manager walked all the way to the HR room, introduced herself to the woman who applied for the job, and then walked her all the way back to her floor for an interview. Once they reached her office, she sat down to start the interview.

Suddenly, the woman spoke up and said, "I just want to tell you up-front that I'm probably not going to take this job, but I'd still like to see what you can offer me." The interview ended very quickly after that!

The nurse manager laughed as she told me, "The walk down to my office lasted longer than the interview did." Obviously, the woman did not get the job (or even an offer).

If you are interviewing for a position, act like you want the job! It doesn't matter if you have several job offers already, or if you don't even really want the job. Act like you want the job!

If you go in acting as if the nurse manager is simply bidding on your labor, then forget about it. If you go in acting as if this isn't where you really want to work, then the interviewer will realize that too, and you probably won't get an offer.

Here are more tips to help you succeed in your interview.

Tip #1: Timing is Everything

First, try to show up ahead of time. I think it would be a great idea to get there 30-40 minutes early because this will help you avoid issues like car trouble, traffic, unexpected delays, etc.

Most hiring managers will not be impressed if you are late to your interview. That will likely give them a negative first impression of you.

Once you are there, you can always wait in the car until you're ready to go into the building. This gives you time to review your resume, turn off your cell phone (important!), practice some interview questions silently, and prepare mentally.

Enter the building about 10-15 minutes before the scheduled interview. I usually start to make my way in about 15 minutes early because it can take a few minutes to find the office and let them know you are there.

You'll want to be in the office/area at least 10-15 minutes before the scheduled interview (this helps to ensure you're early in case their clock is faster than yours). Let the receptionist or office manager know that you are there and that you have an appointment for an interview.

Tip #2 Have Manners

1. Make sure to smile often, and use professional language.

2. When the interviewer comes out, stand up to greet them. Introduce yourself by saying, "Hello, I'm [your name]. It's nice to meet you." Make sure to smile and give a firm handshake while making eye contact with them, though handshaking may not be appropriate during pandemic times (use discretion).

3. Don't sit down in the chair until they've asked you to have a seat.

4. Don't make any assumptions. In other words, don't just hand them your resume, but instead you may simply ask, "I brought a copy of my resume and nursing portfolio if you would like to view it."

5. Let the interviewer control the interview. It's best to sit there, smile, and answer each question as best as you can. Save any questions until the end when they ask, "Do you have any questions?" Don't overdo the questions.

6. Avoid chewing gum. You can use it before the interview in your car, but make sure to spit it out beforehand.

7. Make eye contact regularly, and if two or more people interview you, address each person.

8. Turn off the cell phone or put it in airplane mode.

9. Use good posture. Sit up straight in your chair, looking at them attentively with a slight smile.

10. Don't make it seem as though salary is the only reason you want to get a job.

11. Don't get into an "um" or "like" cycle. Most people use speech disfluencies when they are nervous. They will tack on the word "um" or "like" after things they say. For example, a person may say, "Um, I really like nursing, and um, I think this is a great place to work, and um..." This is where practicing some mock interviews with your friends/family can really help.

12. Don't fidget; Try to sit still. Don't tap your foot, twiddle your fingers, keep adjusting your position in the chair, or anything else. Try to be as calm and still as possible. You want to appear comfortable, relaxed, and confident.

13. Pay them one honest compliment or make one connection with them if you can. You have to be careful, however, because you don't want to seem as if you are a fake and just trying to flatter them.

14. Avoid touchy topics, such as politics, religion, etc.

At the conclusion of the interview, ask any questions you may have. If you don't already have it, try to get the interviewing manager's email or phone number (this is for the follow-up you'll do later).

Then, shake their hand again (if appropriate), tell them it was very nice meeting them, and thank them for giving you the opportunity to sit for the interview. Let them know that you are very interested in the position and that you look forward to hearing more from them.

After the Interview: Make Sure to Follow-Up

There is always the possibility that the hiring manager will offer you a job on the spot, but at most large organizations, they will interview at least 2-3 people before making the decision, even if they loved you.

At my local hospital, they have to give a certain number of interviews and leave the job opening public for a set number of days. It's mandatory.

Therefore, they can't hire a person on the spot, even if they wanted to do so.

If they tell you that they have more interviews to do and they will "let you know," what should you do next? It is recommended that you follow-up after the interview.

I never "followed-up" when I interviewed for my first job as a nurse, but I did still get the job. After I learned about following-up (when applying for my next job), I did it, and I got that job too (which was a much more competitive position). Having done both, I definitely recommend following-up.

How to Follow-Up

First, I only recommend following-up one time. Some experts suggest you should do it up to 2-3 times. However, in the healthcare industry (and especially as an entry-level nurse), I feel that one time is sufficient. You don't want to nag them.

Next, email is the best way I have found to do it. Why email? We live in a digital age, and a letter in the mail just seems a little dated. Email is just easier. If email isn't an option, then a mailed letter/note is the next best option. Calling them directly can interfere with their busy schedule.

People don't like interruptions, and doing so may actually annoy them to the point that they write you off. Therefore, I would personally never call or do it in person for that reason.

When should you send the email? It depends. If they tell you they have to wait 3 weeks to make a decision, you may want to wait a week or so. If they say they'll let you know by the end of the week, do it within a day or two after the interview. If you haven't heard from them after about 1-7 days, I'd definitely consider sending them an email.

You want to make it brief. Make sure to write it in a professional format (not text message slang). Be certain you use proper spelling and grammar.

On the next page is a brief sample of a follow-up email.

Dear [Interviewer's Name],

I just wanted to send you a quick email to thank you again for allowing me the opportunity to interview for the position. I am still very interested in this position, and I would love the opportunity to join your team.

If you have any additional questions or concerns, please let me know.

Thanks again for your consideration,

[Your Name]
[Your Address]
[Your Email]
[Your Phone]

Negotiating a Salary

Whether or not you want to negotiate a salary will depend a lot on the job description itself. Some job listings will say something like, 'Salary is based on experience.' Other times, a set salary/hourly rate may apply for the position, and it really isn't up for negotiation at all. In fact, they may post the hourly/salary rate up-front.

Therefore, my advice is this: Negotiate your salary only if one of the following applies:

- Negotiate if they say up-front that the salary is dependent upon your qualifications, experience, etc. This means there is room for negotiation. Of course, you'll need some experience or qualifications to justify your requested salary.
- If there is an extreme shortage of people for the position and you are the best candidate applying, then you may want to negotiate.

If you are a new nurse graduate, you probably won't have a lot of room for negotiation, and you'll probably have to take what you can get. Most nursing positions want you to have 3-5 years of experience, and while new nurse graduates should be able to secure employment right away, it can still be a challenge to sell an employer on your lack of experience.

If, however, you have years of experience, negotiation may be in order.

You'll just have to evaluate the job listing, your experience, and make a decision about whether or not to negotiate your salary.

I didn't negotiate when I got my first job because the economy was beginning to go down, I knew I had no experience as an RN, and I desperately needed the job so my husband and I could buy our first house. I was adamant about finding a job as quickly as possible, so I wasn't picky.

If you decide to negotiate, you may want to get some salary statistics for the local area, or even ask other nurses working in the same facility.

This will give you a figure to go by. Also, take your nursing portfolio and be prepared to "sell" the employer on why you are worth that amount.

Here's how I would recommend presenting the salary negotiation:

Nurse Manager: What are your salary requirements?

You: Most of the nurses in this area with my level of education and experience earn around $60,000-70,000 (actual salary will vary per area). I'd like for my salary to fall within this range, as I know I'll be a valuable asset to your team.

Alternatively, you could state a specific dollar amount that you are seeking, such as, "Given my experience, credentials, and hard work that I know I can bring to this team, I'm seeking $XX,XXX per year (or $XX.XX per hour).

Reviewing Job Offers

After you've interviewed for the position, you may have to wait a few days (or even a couple of weeks) to hear a response. In most cases, the hiring manager will extend a job offer to you. The job offer will often include the salary offered (or hourly wage), and you usually have a few days to accept or reject the offer.

Make sure you really want the job before you officially accept it because it is very draining having to switch from one company to another, or even one position to another. You'll have to fill out paperwork, go through orientation, and much more.

One other thing you may encounter is the issue of "sign-on bonuses."

These are often bonuses offered if you agree to work with the company for a certain number of months or years. While these often sound very generous (i.e. $5,000 sign-on bonus), in reality, they are not as good as they seem.

I asked a friend about the sign-on bonus she received, and she informed me that it was in the form of an extra $100 per pay period, spread out over 2 years. That's not to say that $100 is not worth it, but it certainly doesn't make as big of an impact as receiving an actual $5,000 up-front.

When I accepted my first job, I was not given a sign-on bonus. Only later did I realize that the hospital used to offer them for my position, but they had to make budget cuts right before I was hired on.

Companies usually offer these bonuses if they are experiencing a severe nursing shortage, or if the position has a very high turnover rate. Nevertheless, always review the terms carefully, and think long and hard before you make a decision to accept any job offers.

Chapter 8:

Succeeding at Your New Job

It can be difficult transitioning from nursing student to new nurse. There are a lot of new things to learn, and it can be overwhelming. Once all the excitement of having a new nursing job begins to settle, it is now time to focus on succeeding at your new job.

The good news is that there are many things you can do to make this transition easier. Here are some tips to help you grow in your new position.

Setting Things Up

- **Orientation:** This is the opportunity for you to get to know important aspects of the job. Orientation takes place before the first day that nurses actually perform job-related duties. You'll be able to work alongside an experienced nurse who will detail various aspects of the job, such as work areas, break areas, and supply areas, as well as discussing job expectations. Orientation also allows you to ask questions or voice your concerns.
- **Nurse Residency:** If the place you go to work has a nurse residency program, I highly recommend you sign-up for this program. It may be required by your employer, as it was in my situation. This program helps you transition from student to nurse. I would compare it to a condensed form of nursing school but with a major focus on clinical skills and preparation. In my program, I was placed in a group with other new nurses who were going into the same specialty. For several weeks, we had in-depth training about cardiac disorders and worked on various cardiac floors and testing centers. This helped us prepare for the types of patients we'd be receiving on our units. It was a great program.
- **Investments:** Most facilities offer retirement investment opportunities, such as matching 401K and mutual fund packages. A great rule to follow is to always set-up your 401k to maximize your employer match. This is essentially free money they offer you as a part of retirement, so make sure to contribute enough to get their full match!
- **Benefits:** Most facilities offer benefit packages that can include health, dental, vision, disability, life insurance, etc. Benefits vary by job location, so it is important that you ask questions about their

benefits and to set them up as soon as possible. It is a good idea to have a list of questions prepared before you attend orientation and benefit meetings so that you can make the most of your opportunities.

Adapting to the Job Atmosphere as a New Nurse

As a nurse, you can potentially work in a variety of settings. For example, many new nurses go to work as a bedside nurse in a hospital, while other nurses may work in a medical clinic, long-term care facility, or rehab center (just to name a few).

The type of job atmosphere you experience depends on the employment setting you choose. For example, a bedside nurse in a hospital has a job that requires extensive standing, bending, stretching, and walking on a daily basis. Therefore, you'll want to learn how to cope with the stresses of the job atmosphere you choose.

Here are some tips that helped me cope with the transition of working 12-hour shifts on a hospital floor.

- **Compression stockings:** These are special "socks" to help prevent leg fatigue. They help compress the legs and keep blood flowing properly. They come in a variety of lengths (thigh or calf-high) and compression grades. I've used 20-30 mmHg, and they've worked great. They may even help prevent varicose veins.
- **Packing snacks:** It's essential you keep fuel in your body so you can survive your shift. Nuts, granola bars, and pouched snacks are easy to access and eat. Many times you don't have regular breaks to sit down and eat. Oftentimes, I've had to pop into the breakroom for a second, eat, and then return to the floor. So, be sure you have snacks that you can easily access.
- **Comfortable shoes:** Get a pair of shoes that you find comfortable. Everyone's foot is different, so I don't really like to recommend a certain brand. I know some nurses love Dansko clogs, while others like Skechers. Some even prefer off brands. Just go to the shoe store and try on a bunch. As a side note, I have found that shoe inserts work great and can usually make any brand more comfortable.
- **Hydration:** Staying hydrated is extremely important! Keep a water bottle accessible, and make time to take drinks. If you become dehydrated, it will affect your energy.
- **Take breaks:** In some healthcare facilities, it is difficult to take a break on time (if at all). However, nurses need to have time to sit, recharge, and eat. If your facility doesn't offer regular breaks, build a buddy

system with your colleagues so that you can all have time to eat. When I was a new nurse, I made the mistake of thinking I could just push through and avoid taking a break because I was so worried I wouldn't finish my tasks. I quickly learned not to do that!

In summary, it may take you time to adapt to whatever job setting you choose. However, things do generally get easier with time. Working 12-hour shifts may seem daunting (if you choose that type of schedule), but it actually goes by pretty fast. In time, your body will usually adapt to the new stresses.

How to Delegate Tasks to Other Staff When Needed

One important aspect about being a nurse is learning to delegate tasks to others. This may come naturally to some people, but others may be shy and do not enjoy this aspect of the job. However, keep in mind that nursing is a team effort, and you can't possibly do everything yourself, especially when things get chaotic.

Here are 5 Rights of Nursing Delegation from the National Guidelines for Nursing Delegation:

1. **Right Task:** As the nurse, can you actually delegate this task? Is this task within your scope of practice to delegate to the LPN or UAP (unlicensed assistive personnel)?

Or is this a task only the RN can do? Make sure the task doesn't require critical thinking or assessment, planning, evaluation, or teaching! Or a helpful reminder I created is, "Does the task require TAPE?". If so, don't delegate it!

What does the **TAPE** acronym mean? It's the tasks that cannot be delegated by the RN. The registered nurse must do it.

- **T**eaching
- **A**ssessment
- **P**lanning
- **E**valuating

Some factors that you need to keep in mind before delegating a task as a registered nurse is your state's and facility's protocols.

2. **Right Circumstance**: look at what is going on with the patient (are they stable or unstable). If the patient is unstable, always do the task yourself. Never delegate it.

Also, assess the current workload of the person to which you are delegating. Are they stretched thin, and it would be too much on the person to ask them to do the task? Don't delegate it!

3. **Right Person**: Are you asking a person who has demonstrated competency in this task? Do they know how to complete this task because they have done it before, and is it within their scope of practice deemed by your state and facility's protocols?

Note: if the person has never done the task before, you will need to either do it yourself or be right there with them as they do it. Remember, even though they can technically do the task, you should always make sure they are competent to do it. You are still accountable for the task!

4. **Right Direction/Communication**: Are you explaining in a very clear way how to perform this task, and what to expect (or report back to you)?

5. **Right Supervision**: Always follow-up with evaluating and supervising how the task was completed, and ensure it was performed correctly. Again, you are accountable for the task!

Source: Barrow JM, Sharma S. Five Rights of Nursing Delegation. [Updated 2023 Jul 24]. In: StatPearls [Internet]. Treasure Island (FL): StatPearls Publishing; 2023 Jan-. Available from: https://www.ncbi.nlm.nih.gov/books/NBK519519/

5 Common New Nurse Mistakes to Avoid

When you first enter the nursing profession as a new nurse graduate, it's easy (and common) to make mistakes on the job. It happens to the best of nurses.

Thankfully, you'll learn how to avoid the common pitfalls of the nursing profession as you gain experience. Nevertheless, there are some mistakes you can avoid from the start.

Mistake #1: Failing to Think Critically

One mistake that new nurses make is that they will often become so focused on completing tasks that they forget to think critically. Although 12-hours seems like a lot of time to complete tasks, nurses are constantly busy administering medications, answering call lights, calling doctors, and so forth.

As a result, it's easy to become focused on completing tasks out of fear of not being able to complete them on time. Therefore, new nurses often fail to take the time to think critically about the medications they are giving and the status of their patients, which is one of the most important aspects of the job.

I once worked with a new nurse who had made this exact mistake. A doctor came storming into our unit, asking which nurse was responsible for the patient in a certain room. The nurse replied, "I am." The doctor then proceeded to tell the new nurse that she was giving the patient both a heparin drip and a enoxaparin injection, which was unnecessary since they were both anticoagulants.

What had happened was that a physician ordered the enoxaparin injection without first discontinuing the heparin drip. Since the new nurse was focused on the task at hand, she didn't stop to consider that the doctor might have made a mistake, and that the patient shouldn't be receiving both types of anticoagulants.

Thankfully, the situation was quickly remedied, but it's important to remember that doctors do make mistakes. As a nurse, you always have to double-check orders and think critically.

Mistake #2: Social Media Problems

Another mistake that new nurses make is that they will post sensitive patient information on social media such as TikTok, Instagram, or Facebook. HIPAA and other privacy laws prohibit the sharing of patient information, and many nurses have been fired for revealing sensitive patient information, taking selfies with patients, posting controversial memes, and so forth.

In addition, new nurses can get into trouble when they spend too much time text messaging or checking their social media accounts. If something were to happen during your shift, they might investigate your social media activity. It wouldn't look good if you were posting 10 times per hour while your patients needed care.

Therefore, you'll want to think twice before you go to social media to take a selfie of a patient, reveal celebrities you saw on the job, or post too often during your shift. It's best to avoid it altogether while on the job.

Mistake #3: Getting Caught Up In Gossip, Cliques, or Drama

As a new nurse, it's only a matter of time before coworkers attempt to gossip with you about the boss or other coworkers, or win you over to their clique. As a nurse, you want to remain neutral, be on friendly terms with everyone, and avoid the politics of your nursing unit.

If you do gossip, know that it can come back to haunt you, and you can end up destroying relationships or causing unnecessary drama with team members.

When someone would approach me to gossip about another coworker, I tried to brush it off, change the subject, or busy myself with some task. Avoid the temptation to slander or gossip about a fellow coworker, even if you feel they deserve it.

As a nurse, I believe it is important to remain as neutral as possible and to maintain a professional attitude.

Mistake #4: Time Management Issues

It can be difficult to complete all of your tasks on time during your nursing shift, and if you don't take the time to learn some simple time management tricks, things will only get worse.

Here are some quick tips on time management:

Ask the right questions in report! This helps get your day started off right and eliminates surprises. When receiving hand-off report, make sure you ask about what procedures the patient will be having, lab times (especially for cardiac enzymes), and special treatments (wound care, central line dressings changes, IV changes, or tubing changes).

These tasks need to be planned out by you so that you can dedicate time to complete them along with your other tasks. Write all this on your report sheet!

Create a sheet to help you keep track of your day after report so you can see how the day will flow! Write down medication times (when you plan on giving them), which patients need special treatments or are going for procedures, possible discharges, and doctors' orders that need to be completed during your shift!

Set goals for when things should be completed! For instance, say that you start your day at 0700. Set a goal that by 0900 you will be done with your morning assessment charting and will start pulling medications for the 1000 medication pass.

Then by 1130, your goal is to be done with your medication pass and get caught up on any new doctor's orders that have come in from morning rounding.

Try to streamline medication administration times! You will spend a lot of time giving medications as a nurse, and if you aren't careful, this can put you behind.

Always check with your institution's policy for medication administration time frames, but try to group medications together.

For instance, 1000 is a big med pass time for day shift (most places allow you to give them 1 hour before and 1 hour after the time they are due). Let's say your patient has meds at 1000 and 1100. In that case, you may be able to give the medications at 1000 so you don't have to go back at 1100 and give them again. However, be sure to watch your time sensitive medications and other similar situations.

Don't just utilize medication passes for giving medications, but do other tasks as well! Don't just give medications but group your tasks together for each patient.

For instance, if a patient needs medications at 1000, but also needs a central line dressing change, IV tubing change, bath, linen change, and to get into the bedside chair, then do all this at once while in the room. This way, the patient will be set for a while, and you can get some other tasks done.

Take it hour by hour, and don't get overwhelmed by thinking about everything you have to get done! Try to stay calm and collected, and get your tasks done one at a time. Don't think, "Oh, it is already 1300, and I haven't even done this," because stressing doesn't help you get them done any faster.

Experience helps with time management! Remember, experience helps with time management, so things will get easier in time! The reason a lot of new nurses get behind is because they are not used to performing skills (which become sharpened with repetition). Therefore, they spend more time than normal starting IVs, giving certain medications, etc. However, as they hone their skills, they will work much faster.

Still in nursing school? If you can, I recommend getting a job as a nursing assistant/intern to help you learn how to develop a routine. This helped me a lot because I knew how the day would flow, and this allowed me to transition easier into the nursing role.

Mistake #5: Putting Too Much on Your Plate

It can be so exciting to finally graduate nursing school, pass NCLEX, and begin working as a nurse.

However, it's easy to overextend yourself and then quickly burn out. I've seen some nurses do this very thing, and they ended up quitting the profession after only a few months.

As a new nurse, you'll want to allow yourself time to adapt to the profession. You'll be going through orientation, taking addition certifications or courses, and learning the ins and outs of the profession.

You definitely don't want to sign up for overtime or extra shifts if you are struggling, as this can quickly lead to burnout when coupled with all of the other stresses of adapting to a new job.

I'd recommend taking it slow for the first 6-12 months on the job. Once you have developed a good routine, have become used to the types of patients you receive on your unit, and have improved your nursing skills and time management, you can ease into adding more work (if you feel compelled to do so).

3 Common New Nurse Struggles

It can be very stressful transitioning from nursing student to nurse, and new grads entering the workforce can battle a whirlwind of emotions. Here are three common struggles new nurses face.

New Nurse Struggle #1: Exhaustion

When I graduated from nursing school, I began working immediately. I couldn't work as a registered nurse until I passed NCLEX, but I had already secured a job in a hospital. My husband and I were also very tight on money at the time, so we really couldn't afford a vacation. Therefore, I went straight from nursing school (and all the work and stress that entailed), to NCLEX, to my new job.

It was pretty intense and exhausting. Once I started working at my new job, I had to go through a nursing residency program, which is like nursing school all over again, as I've already pointed out. I had to take exams, complete competency check-offs, take classes, and of course, work.

I can remember that everything was moving at lightning speed, and I was learning all of this new information. I was utterly exhausted, especially since I hadn't really recovered from nursing school and NCLEX.

But here's the good news for those of you struggling with this right now: Life is about to get so much better for you! After you make it through the transition period, you're going to find that you have so much more free time on your hands.

You won't have to spend your days practicing NCLEX questions. You won't be cramming for nursing school exams. The orientation (or residency) program will soon come to an end, and you'll finally be able to work as a nurse.

And without the pressure of nursing school or exams looming over your head, you'll actually get to enjoy your days off again, too. Oh, and you'll get to do two things on your days off that you probably haven't done much since you started nursing school: Have fun and sleep. Life will feel great again!

New Nurse Struggle #2: Anxiety

Anxiety is also a huge struggle for new nurses, and there are many things that can induce anxiety, stress, or fear. I can still remember many of my worries:

- I would worry that I would make some crazy medical blunder and harm a patient due to my lack of experience or knowledge.
- I would worry that I would call a physician and ask for something really dumb.
- I would worry that I might not hook up medical equipment properly.

- I would worry that my coworkers would think I was dumb or that I wouldn't get along with my coworkers.
- I would worry that I would call a code (or rapid response) when it really wasn't needed, and so on.

It's perfectly normal to feel these things as a new nurse. Here are some things I recommend:

Take advantage of your orientation period! Toward the end of your orientation period (3 weeks before you will be on your own), take the whole patient load without the help of your preceptor, and use your preceptor as a guide (not an extra pair of hands). This is important because you need to learn how to deal with the "chaos" that will be coming your way when you are on your own.

Give it time! Remember, anxiety is normal, and it takes time for it to decrease. Don't beat yourself up if you are having anxiety! Also, if you mess up, pick yourself up, review what happened, and correct the mistake. Sometimes, experience is the best teacher, and you can learn from mistakes.

Find a mentor! Don't "bottle up" your anxiety and keep it to yourself. Many people don't talk about the anxiety they are experiencing because they think it is a sign of weakness (it isn't). So, find another nurse on the floor that you can talk to. You will probably find they had the same issues, which will make you feel better. If there is no one, find a support group or forum online.

A great resource may be found through your local nursing association. Some nursing associations have mentor programs available for new nurse members. In this program, you can sign up to be mentored by an experienced nurse.

Ask for help! You will be doing this your whole nursing career. If you are ever unsure about how to do something or if you need some advice, ask another experienced nurse for help.

Balance your life! Be sure you balance your work vs. play time. Don't pick up extra shifts until your anxiety is decreased and you feel more confident. If you work yourself too much, you will burn out with the job and question if nursing is for you. Also, get enough rest, eat well, and exercise because these things can reduce stress.

New Nurse Struggle #3: Feeling that Nursing is Too Hard!

When you were a nursing student, you worked with a preceptor, and all of the responsibility ultimately fell on that preceptor. However, once you start working as a nurse, the responsibility will fall on you.

If the patient is coding, you've got to take the initiative to provide care. You've got to make sure the meds are given. You've got to assess the patients, and ensure that everything is done before your shift is over.

Therefore, it can be really intense and overwhelming, especially when you're new. (And nursing is hard work!) You might even have a few breakdowns and cry yourself to sleep, wondering if you've made a huge mistake.

However, here's the good news: It does get so much easier over time. You're going to learn tricks that will help you work faster. You'll learn how to document quickly.

You'll also learn nursing time management tips, as I discussed before. You'll learn how to perform nursing skills more quickly as you do them every day. You'll learn where to find supplies.

And it really ties back to the previous points I've made: You have to give it time. At first, it's really hard work and very overwhelming, but you will succeed if you keep pushing forward.

How Long Does it Take for You to Feel "Comfortable?"

I'll share my experience. For me, those first six months were the most grueling. During the first three months, I was in orientation and had a preceptor that I was working with, so I wasn't on my own. It's nice having that person with you because you can ask anything, and you feel more comfortable.

It's still difficult because you're learning the ropes, and you're thinking, "How am I going to get all of my paperwork done?"

After those three months, I was on my own. That's when I began to question myself and wonder, "Can I really do this?" I'd have to remind myself that I had other nurses that I could ask, as well as other resources available.

In fact, when I at the end of my orientation period, a nurse took me aside and said, "Even though you're about to take patients all by yourself, you'll never truly be alone. We're here to help you."

I thought that was so sweet, and it made me feel so much better.

So, you need to remind yourself of that when you have that new nurse anxiety. Remember that you're not completely alone, even when you no longer work with a preceptor.

There was definitely an adjustment period during those three months of being on my own. However, after about a year, I felt so much more comfortable.

In about six months to a year, you'll be comfortable with the skills such as starting IVs, drawing blood, accessing central lines, doing your head-to-toe assessments, charting, giving medications, and talking with doctors.

In time, things begin to fall into place and will become routine. Everything will begin to make sense to you. After six months to a year, you'll feel so much more comfortable. After two or three years, you'll feel like a pro.

The key is to not quit prematurely, but to give yourself time to adjust. When you look back a year from now, you'll be amazed at how much you've grown, and you'll be glad that you stuck with it.

How to Talk to Doctors as a New Nurse

Knowing how to effectively communicate with doctors is very important as a nurse, especially for your patients' well-being.

Many of the new nurses I've precepted were very nervous when they had to talk to a doctor, and they didn't feel confident in communicating the patient's needs or asking important questions.

Therefore, if you are stressed about talking to doctors, you are not alone!

Sadly, many nursing schools fail to teach future nurses how to communicate with physicians, and this can leave new nurses feeling overwhelmed when they are on their own.

In addition, new nurses do not know what is considered "important enough" to report to the doctor, and sometimes fail to notify doctors about certain things.

Here are some tips to help you get comfortable with talking to doctors.

Tip 1: Practice! Practice! Practice!

Don't wait until you are out of orientation and on your own to talk to a doctor about a patient. As a nursing student, you want to practice communicating with doctors as soon as possible, so don't leave this task up to your preceptor!

Once you feel comfortable, I recommend asking your preceptor if you can be the one who calls the doctor about your patient or speaks to them when they make rounds.

Also, observe how your preceptor communicates with doctors. Take notes in how your preceptor approaches a physician and how they deal with any follow-up questions the doctor may have.

The best way to ease your fear when communicating with a doctor is to just jump in and do it. Remember, your preceptor will be there to help you if don't know the answer to their questions. So, if you're still in nursing school, try to make communicating with doctors a priority.

Tip 2: Be Prepared!

Before calling a doctor about a patient or speaking to them during rounds, write down important information about the patient. You will have more than one patient, and you don't want to get them confused.

Write down the following information on your report sheet before calling or speaking to a physician:

- Patient's name and room number
- Why you're calling

- Health history
- Basic labs (CBC, PT/INR, BMP, BUN, creatinine, troponins, d-dimer....anything abnormal)
- Recent vital signs
- Heart rhythm (if known)
- Medications (especially if you are asking about a specific system...for example the cardiac system: say your patient's heart rate is running in the 130s, the doctor is probably going to ask you what medications the patient is taking: beta blockers?....you need to know this)
- Allergies (you don't want to receive an order for something the patient is allergic to and have to call back the doctor and explain that you forgot the patient was allergic to the mediation they just prescribed)

To help you organize the information above, try using the SBAR tool. Many units have preprinted SBAR tools that you can fill out to use before calling the doctor.

The SBAR is a communication method used to promote and simplify communicating important patient information to other members of the healthcare team.

The SBAR method strategically helps communicate a specific patient situation, along with the patient's background, your assessment, and possible recommendations. Really, the goal of the SBAR is to systematize and make communication more consistent.

It helps remove all the fluff and/or unorganized thought that may occur when communicating with others about a patient. Furthermore, it helps the nurse focus on the problem at hand, stay organized, and helps the listener determine what the nurse is trying to convey. And if the listener (like the doctor) has questions about the patient, that information should be easily accessible so the nurse can quickly respond to the doctor's questions.

SBAR is an acronym that stands for:

Situation, **B**ackground, **A**ssessment, **R**ecommendation

Tip 3: Know Who You are Dealing With!

Doctors are just like every other coworker. They each have different quirks about them. Some doctors can be friendly, patient, and provide explanations to your questions, while others can be rude, impatient, and cut you off while you are talking.

As a new nurse or nursing student, you will probably not know which doctors are "harder" to talk to. Therefore, you want to ask other nurses how they communicate with certain physicians, and over time, you will learn how to handle the quirks of each doctor.

Unfortunately, there will likely come a time when you must communicate with a rude doctor. My suggestion is that you just shrug it off, and keep going. Don't let it affect you because you're there to help your patients and to be their voice.

Tip 4: Be Confident, Stand Your Ground, but Be Respectful!

Never be scared or timid when speaking to a doctor. Avoid staring at the ground while talking to them, or speaking in a low tone. You want to show you are confident because many times they can sense when you're nervous, and if they are one of the "rude" doctors, they may try to push you around to test you.

Therefore, be confident, and if you need something for a patient, don't hesitate to ask for it respectfully. For example, if your patient is having shortness of breath and wheezing, and you think they would benefit from a breathing treatment, you would want to call the doctor and bring this to their attention. When you call, you could say, "The patient is having shortness of breath and wheezing. I think they may benefit from a breathing treatment."

This signals to the doctor that you want a breathing treatment for the patient, but it doesn't come off as you are trying to tell them what to do. In other words, if the doctor agrees with you, they will order a treatment.

Now, let's say that you just received an order for a patient, but your nursing intuition tells you something isn't right about the order. I've had this happen before. I had a patient who was not eating or taking their medications, and they were extremely ill.

The physician, who was filling in during the weekend, ordered a nasogastric tube insertion on the patient. However, the patient's recent platelet count was critically low.

Therefore, I called the physician and said, "I see you ordered an NG tube insertion on my patient. I just wanted to confirm the order and let you know that the patient's recent platelet count was extremely low. Do you want me to still proceed with the order?"

Of course, the physician cancelled the order and said he wasn't aware of the platelets. Therefore, if you ever have to question an order, do it with tact. Avoid coming across as condescending to the doctor. We all make mistakes!

Tip 5: Build Rapport with the Physicians!

Establishing a good rapport can go a long way. Consider taking the time to be nice to the rounding physicians and residents. Always try to smile, and ask how they are doing, just as you would with a fellow nurse working the floor with you.

Even if a particular doctor is always grumpy, be kind, and say hello to them when you see them. You may start to see them soften up over time. If you take time to build rapport like this, you will notice that most doctors are easier to talk to and are quicker to respond to your needs.

Here is an example of a potential nurse-to-doctor conversation in which the doctor is being **professional**:

YOU: "Hello, Dr. Smith. I am calling about John Doe in room 805. He came in with congestive heart failure exacerbation. Are you familiar with this patient?"

DOCTOR: "No, can you please tell me about them?"

YOU: "The patient came in yesterday with shortness of breath and weight gain of 6 lbs. over his baseline weight. Dr. Jones started him on IV Lasix 80mg BID, and he has been responding fairly well. However, within the past 10 minutes, he has been having a new onset of "crushing" chest pain. This is why I am calling."

Here is an example of a potential nurse-to-doctor conversation in which the doctor is being **unprofessional and rude**:

DOCTOR: "I swear, if you call me one more time about this patient, you are going to regret it! I can't stand incompetent nurses who think they know everything! I'm going to call your manager and have you written-up."

YOU: "Dr. Smith, please do not talk to me that way. We can talk more about this patient's issues when you have calmed down."

Try to have confidence in yourself, because if you feel uncomfortable communicating with doctors, it will show while you are talking to them. You will start fumbling over your words, and this will convey to the doctor that you are unsure of yourself. Be confident!

If you have questions on whether or not to contact a doctor about your patient's condition, ask the other nurses on your unit. Ask them what they would do. Remember, you are not alone on the floor. You have resources, so use them.

If I Were a New Nurse, I'd Learn These Things ASAP

If I were a brand new nurse or working at a facility I'd never worked, these are the things I would learn as soon as possible.

Protocols, Policies, and Rules

One of the first things I'd want to do is review the protocols for that nursing facility or floor. The protocols will tell you virtually everything you need to know when certain situations arise, and you'll want to be familiar with every type of protocol available.

For example, what should you do if a patient falls? What should you do if a medication error occurs? How should you start certain medications? Your facility will usually address these things in their protocols, so you'll want to be familiar with them.

How do you find the protocols for your nursing facility? They may be located in a binder for you to review, or they may be online through a web portal. Your manager should be able to help you locate them.

I suggest you access your facility's protocols, print them out (if possible), and review them regularly.

Important Document Forms

Another thing I'd want to know is where to locate important document forms. Nothing is worse than being in a huge rush, yet you have to take 5 or 10 minutes searching for some form that you have to complete.

When you first start your job, take time to locate these forms and familiarize yourself with them. That way, when you have to fill out an informed consent sheet or a pre-op checklist, you'll know where to find those forms.

Learn Which Healthcare Providers Go with Each Group

You'll want to be familiar with which healthcare providers work with each group. Many times you'll get new patient admissions, and one patient will be with one doctor group, and another patient will be with another doctor group.

There may be times in which you'll have to get a consult with, say, nephrology, and you'll need to know that this nurse practitioner works with group x, while this PA (physician assistant) works with this other group.

Therefore, it is very helpful if you will simply learn the doctor groups, find out which group works with which group, and commit that information to memory.

Learn the Names of People and Departments

I'd also want to learn the names of people and departments that I'd be calling (or accessing via communication devices like Vocera) regularly throughout my shift.

For example, you'll want to be familiar with pharmacy, supply, lab, transport, respiratory therapy, X-ray, and so forth. You'll be contacting these people often.

In addition, you'll want to know how to use programs (or the phone numbers) to contact these people. For example, let's say you have to order some supplies. You'll want to know how to find and launch the program on the computer (or find the form) to order them.

If you need to transport your patient to a different department, you'll want to know how to use the program to get that done.

When you have time, especially during orientation, play with the software and ask other nurses if you can input the order or open the program so that you will know exactly how to do it once you are on your own.

Crash Cart Location

The location of the crash cart is another important thing you'll want to know as a nurse. I'd recommend finding the crash cart on your unit, and then look through it. Granted, most of the crash cart drawers will be locked, but you can still look through some of the drawers, and the locked ones may be labeled.

In addition, during residency or orientation, there will often be an opened crash cart for you to look through so that you can learn where everything is located inside, which is especially important in case you ever need to find something fast, such as during a code situation.

Supply Closet or Supply Room

Another thing I'd do as a new nurse is find the supply closet (also called supply room). You'll want to just scan the room and make mental notes of where things are located so you can grab them in a hurry when you need them.

For example, where is the IV tubing located? Where is the normal saline located? Where are the supplies to start an IV? Where are sterile gloves?

Learn the Skills of Your Coworkers

Finally, as time goes on, you'll want to learn the skills and experience of your coworkers. Which nurse is really good at starting an IV? Which nurse is really good at nasogastric tubes or Foley catheters?

You may find that there are some nursing skills or nursing tasks that you haven't performed in a while, or some that you don't do particularly well as a new nurse. If you have trouble, you'll want to know the nurse that can help you get the job done.

Chapter 9:

Advancing in Your Career

The awesome thing about the nursing profession is that you have so many ways to grow in your career. Nursing does not stop at the bedside. Some people think that nurses only work in a hospital at a patient's bedside, but this is simply not true.

Not only are there countless specialties in which you can work outside of bedside nursing, but you can also advance to leadership positions or earn advanced degrees, which expand your scope of practice.

Here are some ways you can advance in nursing:

Build Bridges and Network with Others

A vital aspect of climbing the career ladder in nursing is to build bridges and network with others. As I mentioned previously, I've benefited from networking. In fact, this is how I secured my first nursing job.

Networking allows you to get the inside scoop on job openings, specific names and contact information of people who can help you get the job, and develop meaningful relationships that you can carry throughout your career.

Some simple ways you can network include the following:

- Attend seminars/continuing education opportunities
- Join nursing associations and go to events
- Introduce yourself to coworkers in your facility and get to know them
- Sign-up for local community events

As a side note, networking is not only about helping "me, me, me," but also about helping others.

At some point in your career, you may see a new nurse struggling. You can step up and mentor them, help them secure a position, and more. Networking should benefit everyone.

Obtaining Certifications

Another great way to grow in your career is to obtain additional certifications. These can be simple certification programs offered by your facility or nationally recognized certifications.

Local Certifications

Many facilities offer basic certification classes you can take to increase your skills and knowledge. These are usually educational opportunities offered during the week that you can attend, and you must pass an exam to earn the certification.

One of the great things about these classes is that you usually get paid to attend them. And in some cases, you could get a pay increase after completing them.

Some certification classes offered could be:

- ECG Interpretation
- Advanced IV Therapy and Skills
- Ventilator Care
- Advanced Cardiovascular Life Support
- Pediatric Advanced Life Support
- Diabetes and Glucose Management

Nationally Recognized Certifications

Aside from local certifications, you can also earn certifications that are recognized nationally.

For example, once nurses have fulfilled the specific examination, education, and experience criteria, the American Nurses Credentialing Center (ANCC) offers professional certification, as do other credentialing organizations.

A few of the certification areas include the following:

- Medical-Surgical Nursing (MEDSURG-BC)
- Cardiac Vascular Nursing (CV-BC)
- Pediatric Nursing (PED-BC)
- Gerontological Nursing (GERO-BC)
- Nursing Case Management (CMGT-BC)

Professional Growth Programs

Some facilities offer professional growth programs for nurses. These programs require the nurse to complete a certain number of educational and volunteer hours, teaching projects, and other additional work in exchange for a higher annual pay raise.

Earn an Advanced Degree

The minimum requirement to become a registered nurse is to earn an associate's degree, bachelor's degree, or graduate from an approved diploma program. Recent graduates must then pass the Next Generation NCLEX exam.

To become an advanced practice nurse, it is necessary to earn an MSN (Master of Science in Nursing) or doctorate degree. You can specialize in one or more of the following main APRN areas:

- Clinical Nurse Specialist (CNS)
- Nurse Practitioner (NP)
- Certified Nurse Midwife (CNM)
- Certified Nurse Anesthetist (CRNA)

If you ever feel like you are getting burned out in nursing, an advanced degree may be a great option to help reinvigorate you. Not only will you be able to increase your scope of practice, but you will also be able to earn a higher income.

For instance, according to the Bureau of Labor Statistics (BLS.gov), in 2021, a registered nurse earned a yearly salary average of $82,750, while a nurse practitioner earned a yearly salary average of $118,040.

Instead of becoming an advanced practice nurse, you can also earn a masters degree that aids in your nursing career advancement. A few include the following:

- Masters in Nurse Education
- Masters in Nurse Leadership
- Masters in Case Management
- Masters in Infection Prevention

A doctoral degree can open up even more opportunities for advancement and income. A few of those degrees include:

- Doctor of Nursing Practice
- Doctor of Nursing Science
- Doctor of Nurse Anesthesia Practice

Applying for Shift Leader or Management Positions

Advancing to a management position is another way you can grow in the nursing profession. After working as a registered nurse for 3-4 years, it may be advantageous to apply for management positions. There are different levels, and the title varies by the organization.

The shift leader, or also called team leader or charge nurse, is responsible for ensuring the unit is working smoothly but doesn't usually have a patient assignment (unless the unit is short-staffed). They are there to support the staff when needed, develop the work schedule, ensure equipment is working properly, and help with other duties requested by the nurse manager.

Some units even have assistant nurse managers. Their job duties fall somewhere between that of the shift leader and nurse manager's duties, depending on the facility.

The nurse unit manager has the responsibility of ensuring that the best practices are exercised in the nursing unit. The manager is in charge of coordination, leading, evaluating, and planning services within the nursing unit. Many organizations are now requiring an advanced degree in nursing leadership for this type of position.

Other degrees that can help nurses advance in their careers to management positions include the following:

- Health Services Administration
- Public Health
- Long-Term Care Administration
- Public Administration
- Business Management

Chapter 10:

Download Resumes and Cover Letters

To access the resume templates and cover letters that are included with this guide, you **must download them**.

To **download,** visit: https://www.registerednursern.com/bonuses/

Enter the passcode: **xa75galx2**

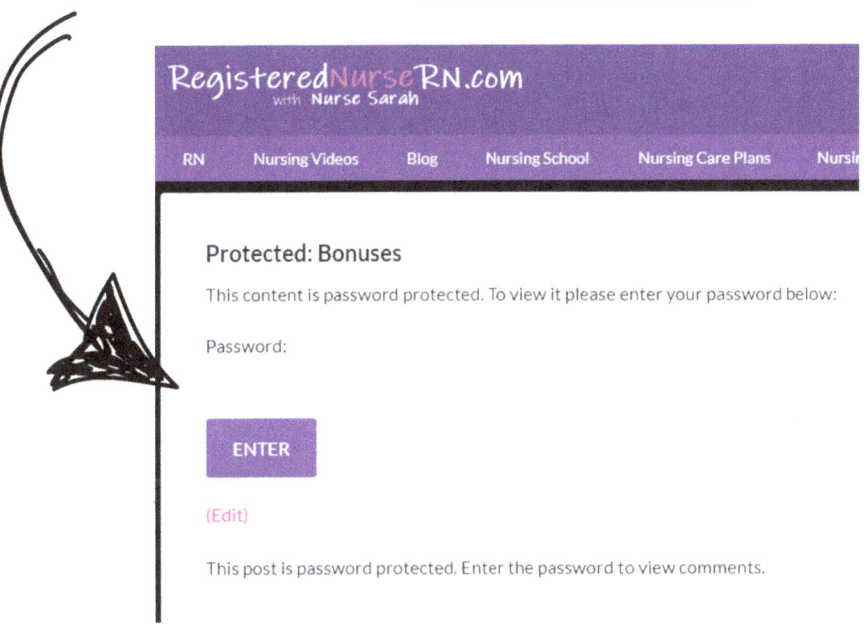

Then click ENTER.

After the download page loads, you will see the names of each resume template and cover letter. Find the template design you want, then download it by clicking the link (usually with the left mouse button).

If clicking the left mouse button does not start the download process, try clicking the right mouse button, which may provide an option called "save target as." Click that to download to a location on your computer (such as desktop or downloads folder) where you can easily find it.

If the download still doesn't start, consider the following:

- You may have a pop-up blocker installed. You may need to disable any pop-up blockers or enable permission for our website so that the download box can appear.
- Try a different web browser. If you are using Firefox, try Google Chrome or Microsoft Edge.

Once you download the individual file to your computer, you can access it right away. If you downloaded the entire .zip file, right or left click on the file on your computer and click "Extract All." This will unzip the file's content.

If you have a Mac, you may need to download an unzipping utility to access the zipped folder. Otherwise, you may prefer to download the files individually in .docx format (instead of the entire content in a zipped folder).

Next, open the unzipped folder to view the various folders inside. One folder will contain all resume templates, another will contain cover letters, and so forth. Open each folder to view the content.

All templates were created in .docx (or .doc) format, which is a format used by Microsoft Word software. For best results, I highly recommend you edit the templates in Microsoft Word. You can usually get a free online version or free trial at microsoft.com.

If you cannot access Microsoft Word, you may be able to use a free document program such as Google Docs. However, if you open them in any other program, some of the formatting may become slightly distorted. For best results and minimal errors with documents, I recommend Microsoft Word.

Using the Resumes Templates and Cover Letters

How do I edit the templates by adding my own information?

Using **Microsoft Word** is the best way to do this. Simply **double-click** the text area you want to change. A box will outline the text after you click it. Then delete, and add your own text. You can even change the font, size, or color to whatever you want.

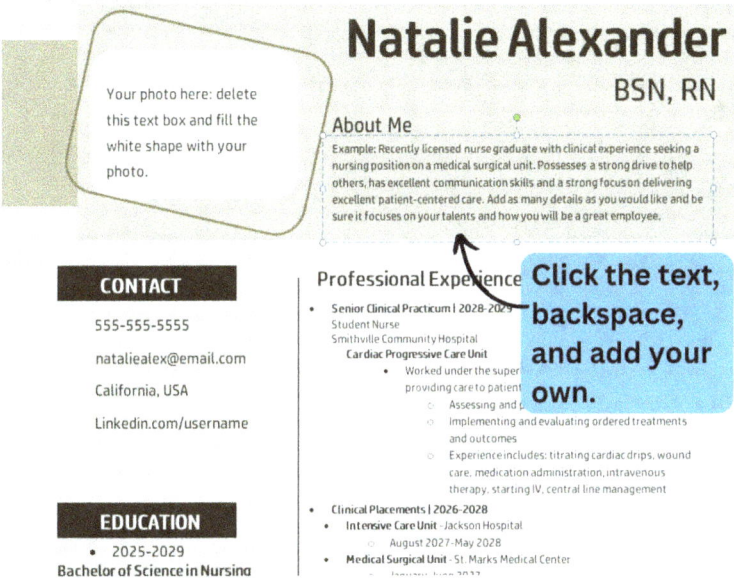

How to change size, font, and color of text?

Select the text you want to change by double-clicking it to highlight it, click **home** on the toolbar, then select the font, size, and color you want.

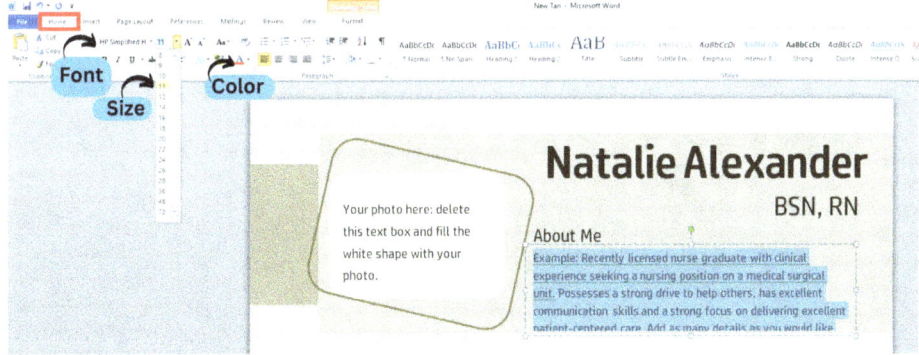

How do I add my own picture to the resume template?

Select a resume template that has this feature (not all of the resume templates allow for picture, so you don't have to include one).

1.**Double-click** the text that reads, "Your photo here: delete this text box and fill the white shape with your photo," and **press backspace** to delete the text. The text will disappear, and a **broken line box** will be around the empty space.

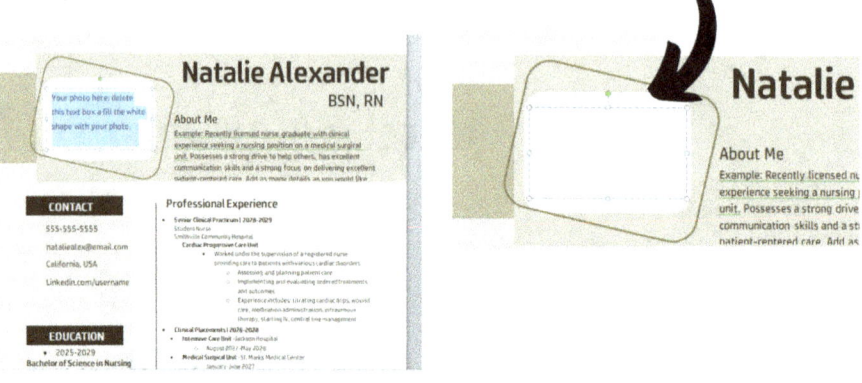

2. *Hover over the broken box with your mouse* and **RIGHT click**. A menu bar will pop up. Go down, and click at the bottom "**format shape**".

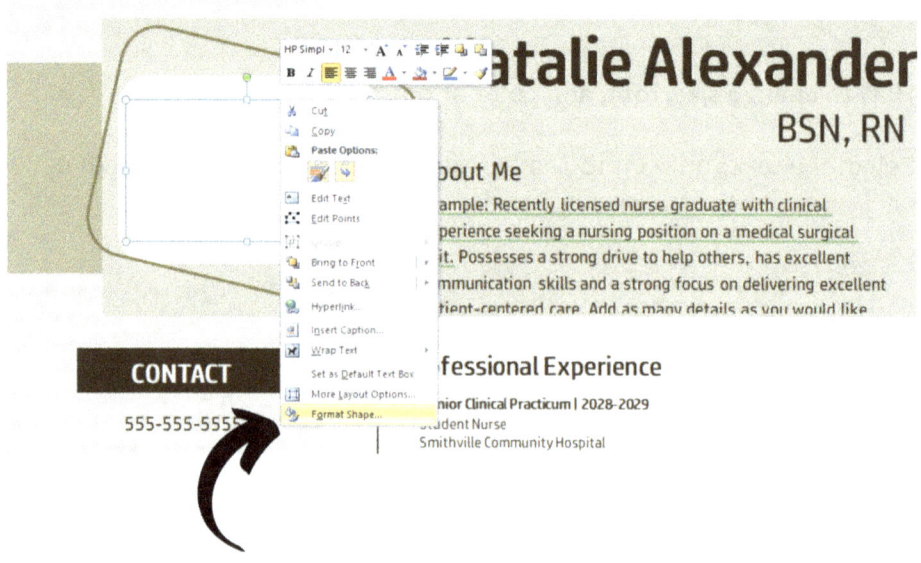

3. A "format picture" box will appear. Click the radio button that says **"picture or texture fill."**

4. Next, click **"file"** below this. You will be prompted to select a picture on your device. Select a picture, and click **"insert"** and then **"close."** Remember to use a picture that is a headshot and will complement the resume.

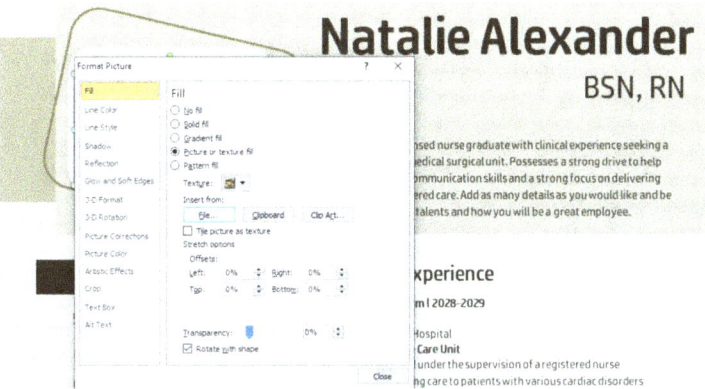

4. Your picture will appear in the space. It will need to be stretched and resized to fit properly, as shown below.

How do I change the star ratings for the skills section?

If you choose to use a resume template that has a star rating for the skills section, you will need to adjust the stars to match your skill level.

To adjust the stars, just click and rearrange to your desired position. You can also click a star and "copy and paste" it to make more of them.

1. To create a star from scratch, click "**Insert**" on toolbar. Then click "Shapes". A box of shapes will appear. Go down to the section that says, "Stars and Banners," and choose the "5-Point Star."

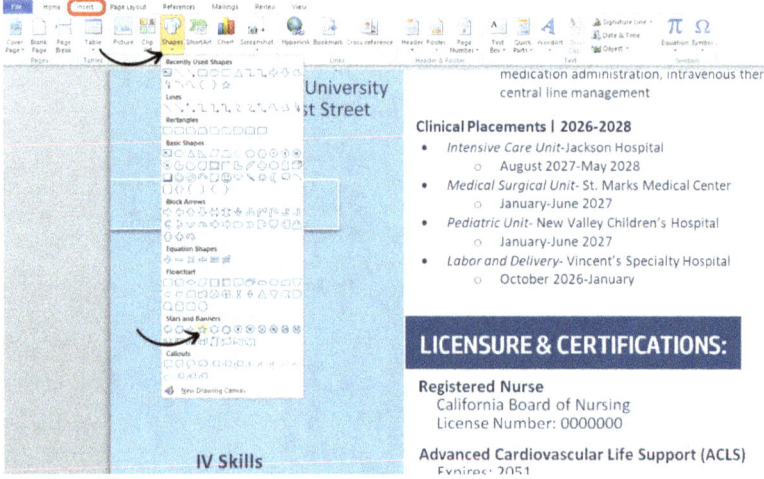

2. Your cursor will turn into a cross shape so you can place the star in the desired space. LEFT-click and hold down to drag the star to your desired location.

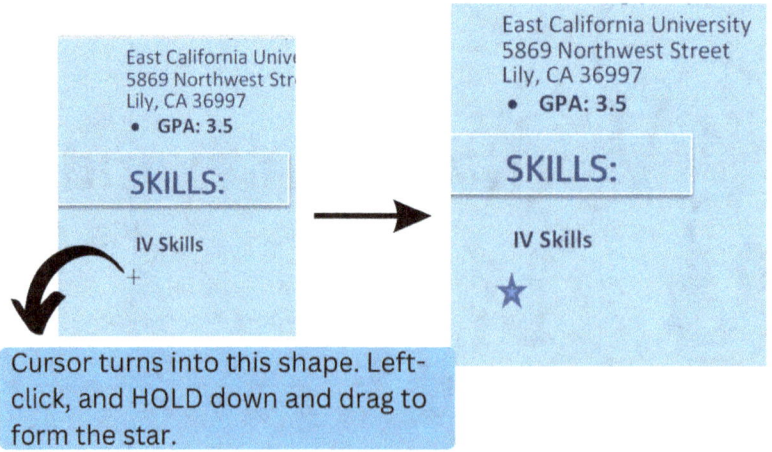

Cursor turns into this shape. Left-click, and HOLD down and drag to form the star.

3. To change the color of the star, click the star, and a broken outline box will appear around the star. Make sure your tool bar is clicked on "Format". Then click "Shape Fill," and select the color white. Next, click "Shape Outline," and click "No Outline".

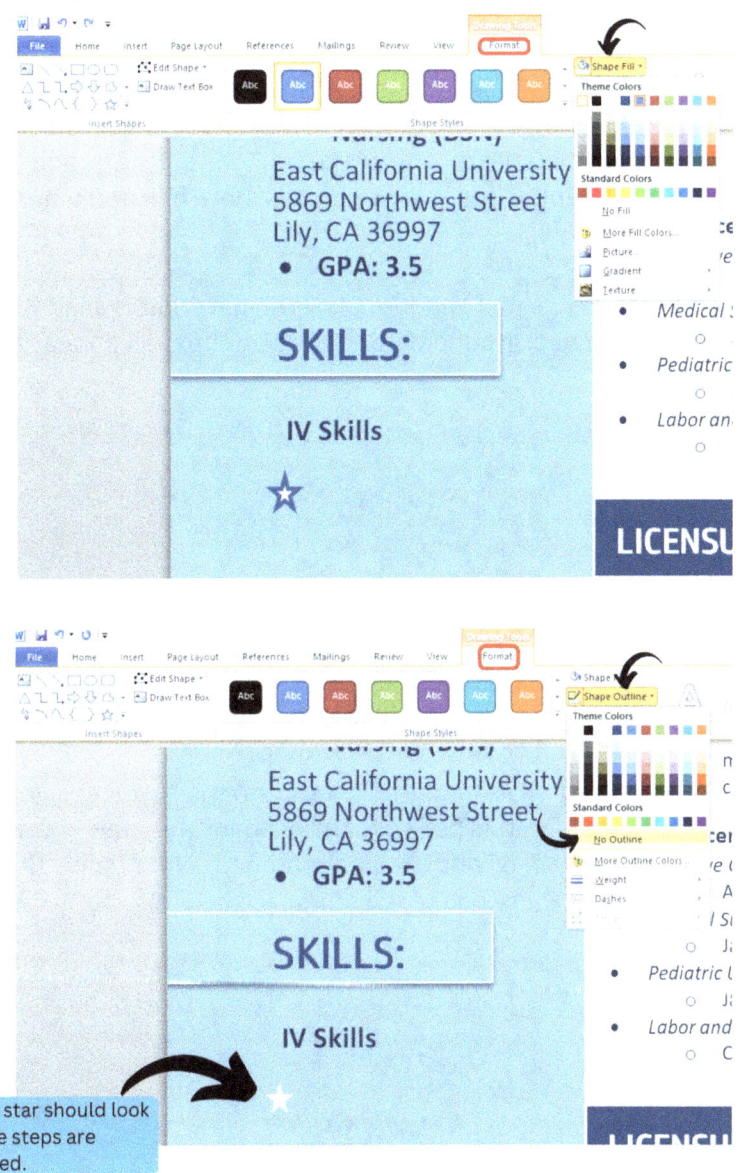

How the star should look when the steps are completed.

To make more stars, you can complete the steps again until you have the desired amount of stars. Alternatively, you can click the star, right-click, and select copy. Then press CTRL and the letter Z to paste the star.

How to make 4.5 stars (half stars)?

In your template, there will be at least one section that has 4.5 stars. Move and rearrange these stars to match the skill you want to highlight as 4.5 stars.

For example, in this skill section, the IV skills has 4.5 stars. However, let's say you want to change it to 5 stars and make critical thinking 4.5. You can drag (or copy and paste) one of the full (or half) stars, and move it to the section you want. If you want to create more half stars, here is how to do that:

1. Find the star that is half shaded. Click the part that is shaded (the part that matches the background color). A broken box will appear around this area.

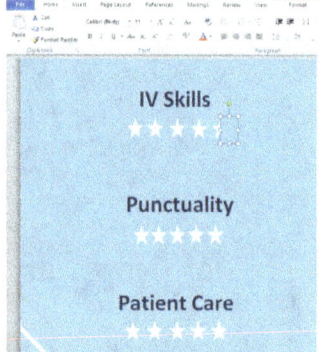

Take this box and drag it up to the 5th star on the "Critical Thinking" section. Then position this box to halfway cover this star. This will make it appear as "half a star" (giving a 4.5 appearance). Note below that the "IV Skills" is now 5 stars (instead of 4.5 stars).

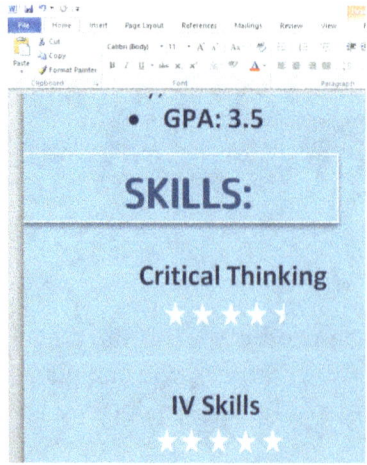

Troubleshooting: Downloading or Editing Your Templates

I can't access the download page in my browser.

Try using a different web browser such as Google Chrome, Firefox, or Microsoft Edge to see if the page loads.

The password isn't working.

Be sure you are entering the correct password: xa75galx2
There are NO capital letters or spaces. After typing in the password, click ENTER. If it doesn't work in one web browser, try a different one.

I can't download the templates.

Make sure any ad or pop-up blocker software is turned off. This type of software will prevent your computer from prompting you to download and save the file.

Where is the file after I download it?

When you download the file, make sure to save it in a place where you can easily find it. The best place would be to select the "Desktop." This is the main background screen on your computer. Many computers automatically save it in a "downloads" folder on your computer, too.

When I try to open the file, I get the following warning: "The converter failed to save the file." What's wrong?

Some people experience the error above when trying to open the document in Word or other programs. To resolve this, try opening the file by right-clicking it, and then select the "open with" option. From there, select Microsoft Word (or other compatible word processing program), and you should be able to open the file successfully.

When I open the file, it was in "compatibility mode" or "read only mode" or "Protected View." What's wrong?

If the file is in "compatibility mode" or "read only mode" or "protected view" then you should still be able to make changes to it. If it says "Protected View," all you have to do is click the "Enable Editing" option that pops up along the top banner of the page.

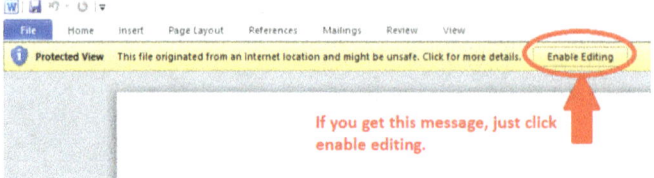

If you experience some other issue, try an alternative program such as Google Docs to see if you can open it in that.

You may need to make sure you aren't saving the files in "read only mode" as a default setting. Even if the file is in "read only mode," you can still edit the document. However, you will need to save it under a new document name when you are finished.

The formatting is not showing up properly on my resume templates, what's wrong?

If you have any issues with formatting at all (such as text overlapping, images being moved or distorted, or other similar issues), make sure the document is actually having an issue, and it is not just appearing that way during editing.

You can view the template by clicking "print preview" on your Word document. Sometimes a file doesn't look like it is formatted correctly, but in reality, it will look fine when it is actually printed. If the document still looks like it is not formatted correctly, make sure you are using Microsoft Word.

Although the templates generally work in other word processing documents that can open .docx files, the best results will be in Word software.

There is a risk of formatting errors when using other word processors, simply because they may not have all of the features or fonts as Microsoft Word.

www.ingramcontent.com/pod-product-compliance
Lightning Source LLC
Chambersburg PA
CBHW072335290526
45794CB00002B/880